Jack Murdock Publication Series on the History of
Science and Exploration in the Pacific Northwest

FIRST OVER THE SISKIYOUS

FIRST OVER
THE SISKIYOUS

Peter Skene Ogden's 1826–1827 Journey
Through the Oregon-California Borderlands

JEFF LaLANDE

OREGON HISTORICAL SOCIETY PRESS

Support for this volume was provided by funds from the M.J. Murdock Charitable Trust as part of the Jack Murdock Publication Series on the History of Science and Exploration in the Pacific Northwest.

Maps drawn by Gary Handschug and photography by Jeff LaLande.

The paper used in this publication meets the minimum requirements of American National Standard for Information Sciences—Permanence of Paper for Printed Library Materials, ANSI Z39.48–1984. ∞

Library of Congress Cataloging-in-Publication Data

LaLande, Jeffrey M.
    First over the Siskiyous

    Includes index.
        1. Oregon—Description and travel.   2. Oregon—History—To 1859.   3. California—Description and travel—to 1848.   4. Ogden, Peter Skene, 1794–1854—Journeys—Oregon.   5. Ogden, Peter Skene, 1794–1854—Journeys—California. I. Ogden, Peter Skene, 1794–1854.   II. Title.
F880.L34 1986   917.95'O43   86-18237
ISBN 0-87595-170-8

Frontis: This view of Mt. Shasta, from the floor of Shasta Valley, shows the northwest flank of the mountain. Peter Skene Ogden saw the peak in December 1826, but never gave a name to it. (Plate XII, "Shasta Butte and Shasta Valley from a point near Camp 70A," in Lt. Henry L. Abbot's report on the 1855 railroad survey, Oregon Historical Society collections, neg. no. 74164)

For my parents
Al and Georgia LaLande

CONTENTS

PUBLISHER'S NOTE   XIII

FOREWORD   XV

PREFACE   XVII

INTRODUCTION   XXI

EDITORIAL PRINCIPLES   XXXIII

THE JOURNEY   I

    SECTION ONE: *Upper Klamath Lake to the
Klamath River Crossing*   3

    SECTION TWO: *Klamath River Crossing to the
Siskiyou Summit*   31

    SECTION THREE: *From Siskiyou Summit to the
Upper Rogue River*   57

    SECTION FOUR: *Down the Rogue River and North
to the Coquille*   77

viii

SECTION FIVE: *On to the South Umpqua and
                      back to the Klamath River*   95

SECTION SIX: *Klamath River to Tule Lake and
                      the Pit River*   111

CONCLUSIONS   121

Territorial Boundaries of the Aboriginal Inhabitants   122

Geographic Names: The Confusing Case of "Shasta"   123

The "Arrowsmith Map" and Early Pacific Northwest
Cartography   126

Blazing the "California Trail"   127

NOTES   131

SELECTED BIBLIOGRAPHY   141

INDEX   145

ILLUSTRATIONS

Mount Shasta	Frontis
Profile of Ogden	XXIII
Fort Vancouver	XXIV
John McLoughlin	XXV
Sir George Simpson	XXVI
"Kanaka Village"	XXVII
Late portrait of Ogden	XXIX
Ogden Journal, 12 September	XXXV
Ogden Journal, 15 [14] February	XXXVII
Williamson River	5
Upper Klamath Lake	6
Upper Klamath Lake	7
Naylox Mountain	8
Swan Lake Valley	9
Lost River	11
Poe Valley	13
Malin	14
Mt. Shasta	15
Tule Lake	16
Tule Lake-Medicine Lake Highlands	17
Tule Lake-Gillem Bluff from Schonchin Butte	18
Devil's Homestead	20
Gillem Bluff-Mt. Dome	20
Bonita Lake	21

Mule deer   22
Klamath Lake "Plain"   26
Klamath River Crossing   27
"Big Bend Canyon"   36
Long Prairie   37
Long Prairie Creek   39
Klamath River-Spannus Gulch   40
Oaks-Beaver Basin   41
Klamath River-Beaver Basin   45
Klamath River-Cottonwood Creek   46
Cottonwood Creek   47
Siskiyou Summit-Cottonwood Creek   48
Cottonwood Creek Valley   49
Siskiyou Summit (N.E. view)   50
Siskiyou Summit (Ogden's "high hill")   51
Siskiyou Gap   52
Oaks   54
Upper Bear Creek Valley   59
Mt. Ashland   60
Bear Creek Valley   62
Bear Creek   63
Lower Bear Creek Valley   65
Rogue River   66
Mt. McLoughlin ("Sastise")   67
Lower Table Rock   70
Rogue River Gorge   73
Rogue River   81
Grants Pass   83
Cow Creek   89
Missouri Bottom   99
South Umpqua-Myrtle Creek   100
Applegate River   102
South Umpqua-Days Creek   105
Applegate Valley   107
Long Prairie   115
Lost River-Stukel Ford   116
Pines-juniper   118
Pit River   119
Upper Klamath Lake-Mt. Pitt   125
Arrowsmith-Hood Map   126

MAPS

Peter Skene Ogden's Route Through the Oregon-California Borderlands,
1826–1827   xxx

Section One   *Upper Klamath Lake to the Klamath*
                       River Crossing   4

Section Two   *Klamath River Crossing to the Siskiyou*
                       Summit   32

Section Three   *From Siskiyou Summit to the Upper*
                       Rogue River   58

Section Four   *Down the Rogue River and North to*
                       the Coquille   78

Section Five   *On to the South Umpqua and back*
                       to the Klamath River   96

Section Six   *Klamath River to Tule Lake and the*
                       Pit River   112

PUBLISHER'S NOTE

THE NINETEENTH was the last great century of interior land mass exploration; in some ways it was the greatest, as the deepest internal secrets
were at last wrested out of Africa and the Americas north and south. Only
the polar regions and splendidly remote ice-coated or jungle-clad islands
remained to be plumbed by the adventurers of our century; these to be
crowned at last by the long-dreamed liftoff into space. From now on, the
oceans and the heavens will further reveal their secrets, but not always
when we choose.

The nineteenth century witnessed a series of evermore deliberate and
exact crisscrossings. Trekkers were followed by explorer-scientists using
principles laid out by the new national academies and the Enlightenment.

The North American land forms were gradually sorted out from the speculations of an earlier century, when redoubtable La Verendrye on the Saint
Lawrence River had estimated concerning the Rocky Mountains, "The
heights can be reached only in the second year after leaving Montreal."

The horizons were moving to the place where Captain William Clark
would carve on a legendary tree at the lower Columbia's Tongue Point,
"By Land from the U. States in 1804 & 5."

When the great eighteenth-century geographer-delineator George
Adams opined to George III, "Geography is in a peculiar manner the science of princes," this thought surely fit in several senses the great continental explorers, including men such as the young American Meriwether
Lewis. President Thomas Jefferson said of Lewis, "His firmness and perseverance yielded to nothing but impossibilities."

Such fine praise must be awarded as well to other seekers within the same generation who solved the riddles and mazes over which we now fly so casually: Simon Fraser, Alexander Mackenzie, Jedediah Smith, David Thompson and his Iroquois guides. Father Silvestre Velez de Escalante, too, followed in the tradition of an earlier friar, the explorer Father Francisco Garces. Among all these luminaries, one must mention the realities of Sacajawea's exceptional contributions to her exploring party.

There is no doubt that in the front rank another, "whose firmness and perseverance yielded to nothing," is included the indomitable Hudson's Bay Company work horse Peter Skene Ogden.

At last, here in the meticulous reconstruction that follows, an author has unraveled for us the arduous southern journey of trapper Peter Skene Ogden into the Oregon-California borderlands. So far as we know, Ogden's was the first journey through and description of this rugged land by an Euro-American explorer. Perhaps it is a bit of lyric, but I believe Ogden had some poetry in his soul, and there would have been certain hours during certain marches when he saw the virgin country around as a sublime engulfment. We are all indebted to Jeff LaLande for bringing this reconstruction to us.

Thomas Vaughan
Oregon Historical Society

FOREWORD

My PLEASURE in Jeff LaLande's commentary on Peter Ogden's 1826–27 expedition is marred only by my regret that Robert W. Sawyer is not alive to enjoy this happy outcome of a project he undertook but was unable to bring to a satisfactory conclusion.

In the spring of 1957, six months after we began our work on Ogden's 1826–27 journal for the Hudson's Bay Record Society publication, Sawyer learned that a rapidly worsening heart condition prohibited him from all field work. There was no one to take his place or to do the legwork for him. As LaLande has demonstrated, on-the-spot exploration is the only way to follow Ogden's geographical clues to his route through the rugged forests, over the rough and broken terrain of southwestern Oregon and northwestern California. Personal observation is necessary to establish even a few decisive reference points. And our deadline was 1 December 1960.

Discouraged but still determined, Sawyer devoted his limited hours of work to the study of maps and records. Shortly before his death in October 1959 he compiled a list of possible locations where Ogden had camped, and urged me to add my own thoughts to his speculations. Some of these provided the basis for the narrative part of my introduction to *Peter Skene Ogden's Snake Country Journal, 1826–1827*, published by the Hudson's Bay Record Society in 1961.

Whatever our shortcomings, we were convinced that the value of the journal itself justified its scheduled publication, and that, once in the public domain, it would impel someone more knowledgeable than we were to correct our mistakes. Jeff LaLande's commentary proves the rightness of our conviction.

In historical research and writing, as in other exercises of the mind, it is only when a statement has been formulated and placed on the record that its assumptions can be tested, its factual bases examined, and its implications criticized. By this manner humankind increases its knowledge and understanding of the problems, great or small, with which it is engaged. To this continuing and necessarily cooperative process that we call "history" LaLande has made a remarkable contribution with this volume, *First Over the Siskiyous*.

Dorothy O. Johansen
Reed College
Portland, Oregon

PREFACE

E VERY PLACE on the globe is unique. The area embraced by southwestern Oregon and northernmost California possesses a special character that sets it far apart, geographically and historically, from the main population centers of either state. It is largely a land of steep mountain ranges—the Siskiyous and others—and deep river canyons, barriers that have deflected most human settlement to more mellow locales. Linked to its peculiar combination of ruggedness and remoteness is the fact that this region, an area virtually unknown to geographers until the second quarter of the nineteenth century, was one of the final portions of the Pacific Northwest to be investigated by fur trappers, the advance guard of Euro-American civilization.

I had never heard of Peter Skene Ogden when I moved from the East Coast to southwestern Oregon in 1969, and I held only vague, romanticized impressions of the Hudson's Bay Company trappers' activities in the Old Oregon Country. Soon, however, an intense interest in local history led me to Peter Ogden's account of his 1826–27 journey through the region. As with most readers, I found Ogden's text confusing and accepted the Hudson's Bay Record Society's 1961 version of his travels without question. But the more familiar I became with local geography, the harder it was to feel certain that the published interpretation of Ogden's route was correct.

In 1981, after an intriguing conversation with a fellow "Ogden buff" (one who was more skeptical of the published version than I), I decided to return, for what must have been at least the fifth or sixth reading, to the 1826–27 journal. But this time I followed Ogden's words without preconceived notions or reliance on the generally accepted version of his itinerary. What ensued were hours spent puzzling over text and topographic maps. I was led up blind alleys, and passed back and forth between geographic plausibility and impossibility. When it finally became clear that Peter Ogden must have passed less than a mile from where I then sat reading his words, my sense of personal connection with the trapper was intense and immediate. It was as if I had suddenly become the first person to visualize correctly the countryside Ogden had described, to follow his actual path through the then-wild land of the Klamath River and Rogue River drainages. After I began documenting the research and writing this book, it became apparent that a few earlier readers of the 1826–27 journal (for example, C. Hart Merriman in the 1920s) had correctly interpreted parts of Ogden's journey through the area, and that much of their knowledge had been mislaid, ignored or forgotten. All interpretations, however, point to Ogden as "first over the Siskiyous" and it now matters little who lays claim to being the first to trace his actual route. More important is the ability we now have to "see" the region through the eyes of Peter Odgen, the first person to write about the unique land of northern California and southwestern Oregon.

≶   ≶   ≶

MANY PERSONS—family, friends, students, and colleagues—have helped me through the several years of this project. To those who have shared my excitement, who have patiently endured my sometimes convoluted explanations of Ogden's travel route, I thank you; your encouragement and support helped immensely.

Marshall Lango, whose skepticism about the "1961 route" initially inspired me to reexamine Ogden's writings, has my special thanks. During treks along the "Ogden Trail" the following persons shared their comradeship, enthusiasm, and sense of adventure with me on various trips to the more remote portions of the route: Claudia Everett, Larry Koster, Fred and Bernice Meamber, Dr. Donald and Dorothy Meamber, Jim and Maryellen Rock, Berta Romio, Jim Vait, and Judy VanTil. Dennis Gray, Janet Joyer, Professor Thomas McClintock, Kathryn Winthrop and Robert Winthrop reviewed an early version of the manuscript and made valuable suggestions. This project grew out of earlier research efforts directly related to my responsibilities as an archaeologist and historian for the USDA-Forest Service. Although the research and writing was done on personal time, because of the topic's relevance to the Forest Service cultural resource management program the initial manuscript was typed, reviewed and approved by the Supervisor's Office of the Rogue River National Forest; Dorothy Newell did the typing. Gary Handschug drew the maps.

It has been a pleasure to work with the people at the Oregon Historical Society, especially Oregon Historical Society Press editor Bruce Taylor Hamilton and the staff. Finally, I am particularly grateful to Professor Dorothy O. Johansen, both for urging me to document and publish this "new" route of Peter Ogden's 1826–27 travels and for graciously writing the foreword to this book.

INTRODUCTION

T HERE WERE PERHAPS a dozen men in the group. Overhead, the leaden
February sky threatened more cold and wet weather. Rain-sodden and
weary from five months on the move, they must have urged their exhausted horses up the steep, forested slope with abundant curses in Canadian patois. They comprised a small advance party of Hudson's Bay Company trappers. Following in their path one day to the rear was the main
group, including Chief Trader Peter Skene Ogden—at that moment a
leader vexed with worries about potentially mutinous employees and hos-
tile natives, a dwindling food supply and a so-far paltry take of beaver
pelts. Would his 1826–27 "Snake Country Brigade" return to Fort Vancouver a failure?

Behind the men, to the south and east, lay their previous trail down the
twisting canyon of the Klamath River. Ahead, somewhere north beyond
the fir- and pine-studded mountain barrier they were now climbing, flowed
an unknown river, one the local Indians had promised would be rich in
beaver. As soon as the advance trappers crested the snow-swept summit of
the Siskiyous, they crossed the pass into the watershed of the new stream.
In doing so, they became the first white men to enter the upper drainage of
the Rogue River.

$$\leqslant \qquad \leqslant \qquad \leqslant$$

BUT AT WHAT EXACT PLACE along the Siskiyou Mountains' "crest" did
Ogden, with his nearly forty French-Canadian and Indian trappers, their
native wives and well over a hundred horses, make this crossing and begin

their descent northwards towards the Rogue? And of larger scope, what was the party's actual route from mid-December, when it left Upper Klamath Lake to reconnoiter the lava beds and shallow lake basins of the northeastern California desert, until early May, when it returned to this same area after nearly three months' wandering among the rugged river canyons of southwestern Oregon? Although such questions may seem to be of relatively minor, antiquarian interest, I hope that the conclusion of this study will demonstrate that the answers do have wider historical significance.

$$\leqslant \qquad \leqslant \qquad \leqslant$$

BORN IN 1794, Peter Ogden was the offspring of middle-class Loyalists who had fled the United States at the close of the Revolution. Growing up the son of a colonial lawyer in Quebec, young Peter abandoned the beginnings of a legal career for a wilder life in the fur trade of the Canadian prairies. When he was sixteen Ogden joined the employ of the thriving, Montreal-based North West Company, then aggressively extending its reach across the continent and harrying the flanks of the older, conservative Hudson's Bay Company (HBC) to the north. During the next decade Ogden saw service at various fur trading posts, from the Great Lakes region to the lower Columbia River. He soon established a reputation as an intelligent, honest, capable, and fearless leader. These traits overcame the Hudson's Bay Company's initial decision not to hire Ogden after it absorbed the competing North West Company in 1821. The "Honourable Company's" reluctance was due to the fact that Ogden had been one of the most fiercely partisan "Nor'westers" during the years of near-war with the HBC fur traders.

Operating out of the HBC's newly established Fort Vancouver during the late 1820s, Ogden led a series of six "Snake Country Brigades." Trapping the largely unexplored intermountain region to the east and south—the Pacific slope of the Rocky Mountains, the Snake River Plain, the Great Basin and the the *terra incognita* situated between the Willamette Valley and the California missions—Ogden logged several thousand miles of travel through the hinterland of the Oregon Country. Due to his aggressive leadership of the 1824–30 "Snake Country" expeditions, Peter Ogden's stature as a regional trailblazer ranks with the reputations of Lewis and Clark, David Thompson, Jedediah Smith and others.

The main purpose of the Snake Country Brigades, however, was exploitation, not exploration. Ogden and other HBC chief traders of this period were carrying out the Company's "trap out the streams" policy. Conceived by HBC Governor George Simpson and implemented by Chief Factor

Profile of young Peter Skene Ogden (ca. 1822), a likeness probably made not long before he left Canada for the Hudson's Bay Company's newly acquired Columbia River region. (Oregon Historical Society collections, neg. no. 407)

John McLoughlin, the idea was to create a vast "fur desert" buffer around the company's rich new territory along the Columbia River, a vast, remote area the British claimed, yet "shared"—by treaty at least—with the United States. By leaving the region's far-flung rivers stripped of beaver, Simpson believed that he would blunt the penetration of American trappers—and that the Pacific Northwest would thereby remain safely in British hands.

Ogden's third Snake Country expedition (which did not reach the banks of the Snake River until the very end of the journey) was meant to trap the streams flowing through the "blank space" on the map, that area situated between the Columbia River drainage on the north and the head-

Fort Vancouver, as painted by H. J. Warre. Established for over twenty years at the time of this mid-1840's view, the fort served as the administrative, economic and social capital of the Hudson's Bay Company's "Oregon Country" empire. This view shows the second fort (built in 1829), located several miles downstream of the short-lived first Fort Vancouver from which Ogden began his 1826–27 journey. (Oregon Historical Society collections, neg. no. 803)

Chief Factor John McLoughlin, able and iron-willed ruler of the "Honourable Company's" Columbia Department during the years of Ogden's "Snake Country Brigades." Both of the men had spent their early careers on the Canadian prairies, working at the remote fur trapping posts of the North West Company. (Oregon Historical Society collections, neg. no. 248)

Sir George Simpson, shrewd governor of the HBC's North American territories, instigated the "fur desert" policy that led to Ogden's 1826–27 foray south into unknown lands. (McCord Museum, Montreal)

Eastward view of "Kanaka Village" (foreground) and Fort
Vancouver (left-of-center, in the distance). The village
was home to some of the French-Canadian trappers and
other employees who made up Ogden's "Snake Country
Brigades." Looking up the Columbia River toward Mt.
Hood, this 1851 view shows the beginning portion of the
chief trader's 1826–27 route: upriver and past the Cascades. (Smithsonian Institution, Bureau of American
Ethography)

waters of the Sacramento River to the south. The sparse geographic knowl-
edge about this land consisted of little more than rumors, and one of these
concerned the purported existence of the great Buonaventura River. The
Buonaventura, thought to flow all the way from the west slope of the
Rockies to the Pacific, was one of the last geographic myths of the Far
West. Incidental to his beaver trapping mission, Ogden was ordered to
search the region for any river that met the description of the fabled
Buonaventura.

Ogden began his foray in the early autumn of 1826 with a full comple-
ment of horses, supplies (including trade items for the Indians he met along
the way), and nearly two score trappers. A few of them were seasoned
Company men like François Payette and Tom McKay, Dr. McLoughlin's
part-Indian stepson and a wide-ranging explorer in his own right. Other
members were evidently new to the trade. To the inexperienced men was

added a number of "Freemen," by most accounts an often reckless and irresponsible breed of trapper that Ogden, though a huge man physically, had to control with a combination of discipline and cajolery. Some of the men were engaged largely in hunting meat for the brigade. Finally, the party included an unknown number of women, the trappers' Indian wives who made themselves indispensable to the expedition's progress by butchering game, cooking meals and curing hides.[1] In short, the brigade, which travelled the country much like a nomadic "village" of mounted Indians (only doing so in mid-winter and through unknown territory), presented a very real challenge to the chief trader's leadership abilities.

≲ ≲ ≲

THE QUESTION OF Peter Skene Ogden's actual 1826–27 route has been the subject of debate ever since an edition of his journal was first published in 1910.[2] This version, edited by T.C. Elliott and based on a heavily abridged copy of Ogden's journal made by Agnes C. Laut during her 1905 visit to the Company's Beaver House archives in London, took many liberties with the journal's original wording. Consequently, it is unusable as a primary historical source. The "Laut-Elliott" version corrected Ogden's spelling, dropped numerous sentences and whole paragraphs, omitted up to eight days of journal entries in succession, and changed the wording of entire sections in order to make them "clear," all without notice to the reader that the published text had been substantially modernized and abbreviated from that of the original. In addition, Elliott included geographic interpretations of Ogden's route that are very much in error.

The situation was partially remedied with the Hudson's Bay Record Society's 1961 publication of the 1826–27 *Snake Country Journal*, a complete, verbatim edition that preserved both Ogden's unique spellings and his exasperating lack of punctuation.[3] However, the editors of the 1961 version included a new interpretation of the brigade's northern California–southwestern Oregon itinerary that, based on a critical reexamination of Ogden's journal, appears also to be wrong. The "1961 route" has the chief trader and his party first reaching the Klamath River near Beswick, California, descending that stream to Beaver Creek and crossing the Siskiyou Mountains into the Rogue River drainage at the headwaters of the Little Applegate River. This version provided very little explanation of most of Ogden's subsequent northward travel. For some readers, the 1961 interpretation of Ogden's route created almost as many new geographic puzzles as the old ones it solved; significant discrepancies existed between the itinerary offered by the editors and the one that can be inferred from Ogden's stated course directions, travel distances and his descriptions of the coun-

This late-in-life portrait of Peter Ogden (ca. 1850) dates to long after his years of hard toil and personal danger in the wilds of the "Snake Country." (Oregon Historical Society collections, neg. no. 707)

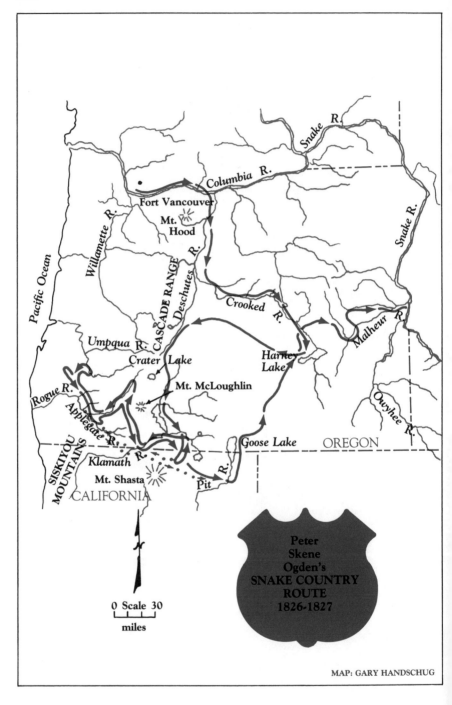

Pacific Ocean

Willamette R.

Columbia R.

Fort Vancouver

Mt. Hood

CASCADE RANGE

Deschutes R.

Snake R.

Snake R.

Snake R.

Crooked R.

Malheur R.

Umpqua R.

Crater Lake

Harney Lake

Rogue R.

Mt. McLoughlin

Applegate R.

Owyhee R.

SISKIYOU MOUNTAINS

Klamath R.

Goose Lake

OREGON

Mt. Shasta

Pit R.

CALIFORNIA

N

0 Scale 30
miles

Peter
Skene
Ogden's
SNAKE COUNTRY
ROUTE
1826-1827

MAP: GARY HANDSCHUG

tryside. Nevertheless, over the past two decades, the travel route given in the 1961 Hudson's Bay Record Society publication has gained wide acceptance, reinforced by its use in the secondary historical literature on the subject—from popular works like Richard Dillon's *Siskiyou Trail* to scholarly monographs dealing with the Hudson's Bay Company.[4]

One hesitates to jump in and "muddy the water" with yet another version of Ogden's travel route. However, the alternative interpretation that follows is offered in the hope of improving our ability to decipher those first pages in the written history of the area, one of the last sections of the Far West to open its secrets to Euro-American explorers.

≶   ≶   ≶

THE FOLLOWING COMMENTARY on Ogden's travel route begins on December "12," 1826, at the point where his "Snake Country Brigade" first reached the eastern shore of Upper Klamath Lake. As Professor Dorothy O. Johansen notes in her introduction to the 1961 edition of the chief trader's journal, the actual date was December 11; Ogden's calendar dates were in error by one day from the beginning of his trip in mid-September until the last day of February (1827 was not, contrary to his belief, a leap year).

The commentary ends on May 7, 1827, when the brigade reached the upper Pit River and turned northeast towards the Snake River and Fort Nez Perce. Neither the initial portion of Ogden's route, from near the Dalles through the high desert of central Oregon to Upper Klamath Lake, nor the final leg of the trip, from the Pit River to the Snake, is in doubt. In brief, the thesis of this publication is as follows: Ogden and his party left Upper Klamath Lake and travelled generally southward into the Lost River-Tule Lake area. After retracing a portion of their route, they first reached and crossed the Klamath River just south of the present city of Klamath Falls and then descended the Klamath to Cottonwood Creek. The brigade ascended Cottonwood Creek to its sources and crossed the Siskiyous into Bear Creek Valley (part of the Rogue River drainage) by way of Siskiyou Summit (near the present route of Interstate Highway 5). The trappers travelled up the Rogue River to near Prospect and then descended it to the site of Grants Pass. Heading northward, the party evidently went as far as the Middle Fork of the Coquille and the South Fork of the Umpqua before retracing its steps southward, with a short detour into the Applegate Valley, to the Klamath River.

For the sake of clarity and convenience, Ogden's itinerary has been divided into six major segments:

SECTION ONE: *Upper Klamath Lake to the Klamath River Crossing*

SECTION TWO: *Klamath River Crossing to the Siskiyou Summit*

SECTION THREE: *Siskiyou Summit to the Upper Rogue River*
SECTION FOUR: *Down the Rogue River and North to the
                          Coquille*
SECTION FIVE: *On to the South Umpqua and back to the
                          Klamath River*
SECTION SIX: *Klamath River to Tule Lake and the Pit River*

At the beginning of each section, the commentary briefly describes that portion of Ogden's travel. More detailed geographic discussion is then provided for each of the relevant daily journal entries.

EDITORIAL PRINCIPLES

THROUGHOUT THE FOLLOWING COMMENTARY, extensive quotations from the 1961 edition of Ogden's 1826–27 journal have been used; these excerpts are reprinted with the permission of the Hudson's Bay Record Society. Due to the unwieldy length and varying subject matter of many of Ogden's daily entries, only those parts of the journal pertinent to Ogden's travel route have been included here. The reader should refer to the 1961 edition for the full text of the journal.

Some explanation of the editorial treatment of the journal narrative is in order. As stated above, Ogden's journal dates were off by one day from the start of the journey until the end of February. The commentary indicates Ogden's erroneous dates with quotation marks; the true calendar dates are enclosed by brackets. Further use of brackets within Ogden's narrative denote this writer's occasional geographical interpretations and other interjections into the original text; parenthetical statements within the journal's entries, however, are Ogden's own. Unless otherwise noted, any emphasis given to words or phrases in the journal's text is also original. Only the less-obvious misspellings in the journal are noted with *sic*.

At the slight but possible risk of changing Ogden's original meaning, obvious sentence breaks have been interpolated between words by placing the symbol ≶ at each location.[5] Ogden's idiosyncratic spelling and his general lack of punctuation have been retained. A three-point ellipsis (. . .) indicates a break within a single (that is, as *orginally* punctuated) sentence; a four-point ellipsis is used for a break between two or more sentences.

"On Monday 12th [of September 1826] I took my departure from Ft. Vancouver." So wrote Peter Ogden on the first page of his 1826–27 "Snake Country Journal." This only known existing copy of the Journal is not in Ogden's handwriting; it is a "clean copy" transcribed by a clerk at Fort Vancouver shortly after Ogden's return. (Courtesy Hudson's Bay Company Archives)

September Monday 19th 1826

On Monday 12th I took my departure from Ft Vancouver in 2 Boats with 12
men bound for the Snake Country and reached the main Dalls of the
Columbia River about 100 miles distant from Ft. Vancouver the fourth
day early and found Mr McKay and party with 100 odd Horses
anxiously waiting my arrival, the Natives altho not numerous are
composed of different Tribes and cause considerable trouble they had
already succeeded in stealing one prime Horse — the day after my arrival
I sent back our Boats under the charge of Mr La Framboise & 5 Men and
wrote to John McLaughlin. The 17th & 18th employed in distributing the
Horses to the Men with their loads — I also wrote to the Gent: of the Interior
and sent off two of Mr Blacks Men with 1100 Salmon conducted by
a party of Men as far as the Falls there they will procure Canoes from
the Natives and proceed on to Ft. McKay thus all being finally settled
and arranged I this morning gave the call to collect the Horses and
rise Camp for my trip to the Snake country or in other words in
quest of Beaver with a party in all 35 assisted by Mr McKay we
found one Horse missing, he was soon after discovered tied in the
branches and shortly after while all hands were busily employed
in loading the Horses Mr McKay discovered an Indian going off with two
which he secured — On leaving our Encampment we followed the banks of
of the Columbia for 2 Miles when we bade it adieu and I must say
altho all appear happy still when I reflect on my last years privation
and sufferings I must confess my sensations on leaving the Columbia
are far different God grant we reach it again in safety and our exertion
crowned with success we followed the banks of a small stream
wooded and rocky for 6 miles and encamped Course from the
Columbia South East — Many of our Horses are rather wild
and threw their loads in the Plains some time was taken
collecting the scattered property Indians are moving about in
all directions, strict watch is kept day and night with the
hopes of saving our Horses — already does our anxiety and trouble
commence the natives are already starving and no doubt will
follow us as long as they can with safety to themselves. The weather
very sultry

A page from Ogden's lengthy journal entry for February "15" [14][1827], the day he sighted and named both present Rogue River and Mount McLoughlin for the "Sastise" [Shasta] Indians. His sentence about "this River I have nam'd Sastise River also a mount equal in height to Mount Hood" begins on the eleventh line. (Courtesy Hudson's Bay Company Archives)

February

untill five in the evening but the distance was not in proportion
to the time from the state of the roads worse they cannot
be the last three days of rain have done them no good
and it is also most injurious to our Trapping from the
water being in such an unsteady state either rising
or falling and it is impossible to Trap to any advantage
This is certainly a fine looking Stream well wooded with
Poplar Aspine and Willows and from its depth it
must either be well supplyed with tributary Streams
or its rise must be far distant we shall in course of time
ascertain it— this River I have nam'd Saslise I have also
a mount equal in height to Mount Hood or Vancouver
I have nam'd Mount Sislise its bearings by our Compass
from our present incampment East South East I have
given these names from the Tribe of Indians who are
well known by all the neighbouring Tribes for the
faculty of Trappers or Traders who may resort to this
Country hereafter by giving english names it often
tends to lead strangers astray, in the Snake Country
my first year I experienced this in regard to many
Rivers— We travelled over a fine level Country
and in reaching this River we saw two small Herds
of White tail Deer they received a salute but
escaped without one being wounded— Distance this
day 15 Miles Course West North West, Beaver 24
Otter 1 —— One of the Trappers reported that
within a short distance of the Camp he met with three
Indians who on seeing him strung their Bows and made
preparations for sending him a few arrows at the same
time making signs for him to leave their Lands he
instantly drew the cover from his Gun and was in
the act of giving them a salute when they took
flight an example must be made of them and
that soon if we wish to remain in the Country

THE JOURNEY

SECTION ONE:
Upper Klamath Lake to the Klamath River Crossing

DUE TO A TOO-LITERAL INTERPRETATION of the direction of travel given in Ogden's journal for December "14," the "1961 version" of his route has Ogden travelling south along the eastern shore of Upper Klamath Lake to the Klamath Falls vicinity. From there his route is conjectured to have passed southeast into the Willow Creek drainage and to have reached the south shore of Tule Lake by heading east (contrary to most of the travel directions and distances given in Ogden's journal entries between mid-December and the end of the month). The sole "original" journal held in the Hudson's Bay Company Archives, however, is actually a copy, *not in Ogden's hand*, and the 1961 edition failed to take into account the likelihood of occasional copying errors, particularly those that would skew such crucial information as compass orientation. This problem was encountered by the editors of Ogden's other "Snake Country Journals."[6]

From Tule Lake, the 1961 route has Ogden returning west, reaching and crossing the Klamath River near the hot springs at Beswick, California. This is the second and most crucial misinterpretation of Ogden's itinerary. Because of its failure to place the chief trader's Klamath River crossing at its actual point, a short distance downstream from the present city of Klamath Falls, the 1961 version's distance points and, consequently, its purported route of travel are much too far to the west.

Taking into account the almost certain December "14" mis-copy of "South West" for southeast, Ogden's subsequent traverse to and from Tule Lake becomes much easier to follow. Via Swan Lake Valley and his Lost River crossing-point near Olene, Ogden travelled south to reach the east

3

4

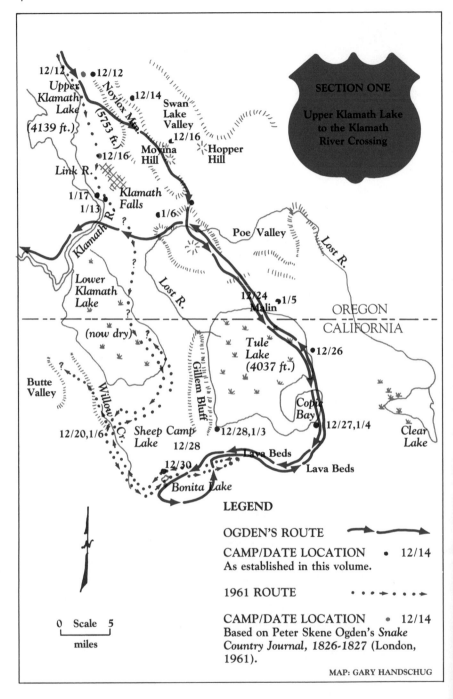

12/12
12/12
Upper
Klamath
Lake
(4139 ft.)
Noylox Mtn.
(5753 ft.)
12/14
Swan
Lake
Valley
12/16
Hopper
Hill
12/16
Movina
Hill
Link R.
Klamath R.
1/17
1/13
Klamath
Falls
?
1/6
Poe Valley
Lost R.

Lower
Klamath
Lake
Lost R.
12/24
Malin
1/5
OREGON
CALIFORNIA
(now dry)
?
?
Tule
Lake
(4037 ft.)
12/26

Butte
Valley
?
Willow Cr.
Gillem Bluff
Copic
Bay
12/27,1/4
Clear
Lake

12/20,1/6
Sheep Camp
Lake
12/28
12/28,1/3
Lava Beds
Lava Beds
12/30
Bonita Lake

LEGEND

OGDEN'S ROUTE

CAMP/DATE LOCATION • 12/14
As established in this volume.

1961 ROUTE • • • ► • • •►

CAMP/DATE LOCATION • 12/14
Based on Peter Skene Ogden's *Snake
Country Journal, 1826-1827* (London,
1961).

MAP: GARY HANDSCHUG

N

0 Scale 5
miles

December "12" [11]: Altho slight rain we raised Camp . . . we crossed over the River.

Leaving the Klamath Marsh village in the morning, Ogden followed the Williamson River (shown here a short distance north of Chiloquin) towards its discharge into Upper Klamath Lake. (Photo by author)

shore of Tule Lake. From the Tule Lake area he backtracked to Lost River, crossed to the north bank and travelled a relatively short, straight route west to the Klamath River, reaching and crossing the Klamath a few miles downstream (southwest) of Klamath Falls. Placing Ogden's December "17" river crossing at this point instead of at Beswick Hot Springs, some thirty to forty miles downstream, not only agrees with Ogden's geographical descriptions up to (and after) this date but also enables one to make a clear and detailed interpretation of his subsequent travel into the Rogue River drainage and beyond. With this first entry the chief trader is on the east shore of Upper Klamath Lake.

6

*December "12" [11]: thence crossing on a point of Land we
soon reached the Lake ⪅ a fine body of water surrounded on
both sides by high land . . . we followed along its banks.*
This northwestward view from near Modoc Point is the
approximate point of Ogden's first sighting of Upper
Klamath Lake. The brigade continued south along this
eastern shoreline, now the route of U.S. Highway 97 and
the Southern Pacific Railroad. (Photo by author)

DECEMBER *"12" [11], [1826]: Altho slight rain we rais'd Camp. . . . we crossed
over the River on starting from thence crossing on a point of Land we soon reached the
Lake ⪅ a fine body of water surrounded on both sides by high Land averaging 1 1/2
miles in width and 15 in length, we followed along its banks and had not onely a hilly
but a stony road and advanced 12 miles and encamped ⪅ the soil along the Lake is
remarkable good ⪅ in one point I saw no less than eight different kinds of wood
amongst the number of soft maples and Hasel. . . . this day no Snow, Course South
⪅ Dist. 12 miles.*

Travelling south from the Klamath Marsh vicinity (where they had visited the "Clamitte Indian Village"), Ogden and his trappers crossed the
Williamson River just downstream from Chiloquin.[7] They reached the
east shore of Upper Klamath Lake, probably at or near Modoc Point, and
continued south along the lakeshore to Barkley Spring. Ogden mentioned
passing "five Huts of Indians" near this place; most likely this was the eth-
nographically known village located at this spring, situated next to the
lake at the foot of the Modoc Rim-Naylox Mountain fault block.[8] Here

members of the party rested for one day in order to dry out their soaked belongings before continuing to the southeast.

DECEMBER "*14*" [*13*]: *Prior to starting this Morning the Indians traded 9 Dogs and 20 fine large Carp—this is certainly a new Fish to me and nearly as good as White fish. On starting we left the Lake [emphasis added] and commenced ascending a very high hill most fatiguing both for man and Horse and most dangerous for the latter owing to some snow which fell last night made it very slippery it was also in many parts*

December "*14*" [*13*]: *On starting we left the Lake and commenced ascending a very high hill.*

This view toward the northwest shows Upper Klamath Lake from the lower slopes of Naylox Mountain. Barkley Spring is located on the flat to the left on this view. Odgen ascended this slope *southeast*, travelling away from the lakeshore. (Photo by author)

December "14" [13]: A very high hill most fatiguing both for man and Horse . . . on reaching the top of the hill we had both a hilly and woody Country.

This southeast view (taken from the same spot as the previous photograph) shows the Modoc Rim-Naylox Mountain-Hogback Mountain fault block that rises just west of the Barkley Spring vicinity (near the community of Algoma, Oregon). Ogden reached the summit of Naylox Mountain (left) and found himself in the hilly pine forest that forms the northwest margin of Swan Lake Valley. (Photo by author)

---

very rocky . . . on reaching the top of the hill we had both a hilly and woody Country ≤ amongst the latter were some fine Cader trees Pines almost of every kind also a wood which strongly resembles Box wood and is onely to be found on very high lands . . . we soon left the Woods and had a marshy Country in advance 10 miles and encamped. Course South West [emphasis added] . . . we had at one time nearly a foot of snow but here we have onely four inches.

The 1961 edition implies (but does not expressly state) that Ogden continued southerly along or at least parallel to the lakeshore to the vicinity of Klamath Falls. This interpretation is based on the journal's travel direction of "South West." A generally south*west* course of travel from Barkley Spring actually would have put Ogden's group somewhere in the middle of Upper Klamath Lake. It is evident that this particular course direction of "South West" must have been a copy error for Odgen's intended "South East." From his geographic description, it is clear that Ogden and his trappers turned southeast at Barkley Spring, *away* from the lakeshore, and climbed the steep escarpment of the Modoc Rim-Naylox Mountain fault block (an elevation gain of about 1,000 feet in less than one mile of horizontal distance). From the forested summit the party continued across somewhat gentler terrain, passing through the Whiteline Reservoir-Cold Springs-Two-mile Ridge area into the northwest corner of Swan Lake Valley (the "marshy Country in advance").[9] Heavy snowfall delayed the trappers' advance until two days later.

December "16" [15]: Our Course South East . . . —the Country level but we have a hilly road before us tomorrow.

This is the southeastward view Ogden would have seen from the level floor of Swan Lake Valley. Hopper Hill (left) and Moyina Hill (right) separate this valley from the Lost River. The distant ridge (center) is located on the near side of Lost River; Ogden passed between the two hills and swung right (west) of this ridge to reach the river. (Photo by author)

DECEMBER "16" [15]: *We had truly a most stormy night . . . but this morning it was clear and cold ≦ we made preparations for starting but from our being buried in the snow it was late ere we did and advanced eight miles and encamped. . . . Our Course South East . . . —the Country level but we have a hilly road before us tomorrow . . . hunters returned. . . , report they saw a fine stream well lined with Willows . . . altho our [Klamath Indian] Guide says there is no Beaver in it.*

Ogden advanced southeast across most of the flat, former Pleistocene lake basin of Swan Lake Valley. The "hilly road" awaiting them would have referred to the view of Hopper Hill and Moyina Hill, which separate the interior-draining Swan Lake Valley from the Lost River drainage to the south. The "hunters," travelling well ahead of the main group, crossed this divide and saw the willow-lined banks of the Lost River in the distance before backtracking to Ogden's camp with this news.

DECEMBER "17" [16]: *. . . at an early hour I sent six men with Traps to examine the River seen yesterday . . . Beaver would be very exceptable to all ≦ we have now travell'd a considerable distance without seeing any and the Trappers for some time past have despaired of ever finding any again. . . . The Trappers retd. in the evening with their Traps, they visited the River for a considerable distance and report it as a large stream well wooded with Willows and Aspine but not the least sign of Beaver nor was there ever any in it—this is truly vexing but I could not pass without examining this River. . . . still I am determined to advance so long as I can prevail on the majority to follow me and how long this will be from their present discontented state I cannot pretend to say.*

Ogden remained at his Swan Lake Valley camp while a half-dozen men went on to reconnniter the Lost River for sign of beaver.[10] The chief trader spent an additional day at this camp while a group of fifteen men under Thomas McKay went off to hunt for badly needed meat supplies.

DECEMBER "19" [18]: *From the dense fog this morning it was 11 A.M. ere we were ready to start and it was night ere we camped. Our course S East distance nine miles ≦ we had a stormy and also a muddy road . . . the late soft weather makes the roads almost impassable ≦ here we are encamped and have a spring of good water . . . grass fine and in advance our Horses will fare well. . . . Mr. McKay informs me we are fortunate in having Guides for had we followed the River [Klamath River] the Lake discharges in we could not have advanced in that direction, the Country as far as the eye can reach being one continued Swamp and Lakes. Some traps set for otters in the River we shall reach tomorrow, the lower part has already been examined and tomorrow I shall send trappers to examine the upper part.*

Odgen's main group crossed the height-of-land south of Swan Lake Valley and bivouacked in the "Pine Flat" area, a few miles west of the present community of Dairy. McKay's group must have travelled southwest from

December "20" [19]: a fine looking stream well lin'd with Willows and had some difficulty in discovering a fording place.
    This eastward (upstream) view is located quite near where Ogden first reached Lost River; his fording place at Olene Gap is a short distance downstream. (Photo by author)

the Swan Lake Valley campsite. Probably climbing to the crest of Hogback Mountain (another of the vicinity's many fault block ridges), McKay would have seen the marshlands (the "continued Swamp and Lakes") of Lake Ewauna-Klamath River-Lower Klamath Lake well off to the south-west. The initially puzzling reference to the "River the Lake discharges in" would, then, clearly indicate that wide, slow stretch of the Klamath River just downstream from Klamath Falls. This is the head of the Klamath River proper, below the so-called Link River (which is actually the start of the Klamath at the outlet of Upper Klamath Lake). The "River we shall reach tomorrow" refers then to the Lost River; at this point Ogden would have had no idea that it flows only as far as Tule Lake, and that it has no connection with the Klamath River drainage to the west.

DECEMBER *"20" [19]: . . . at 10 A.M. we started and advanced six miles over a plain where we reached the river ≶ a fine looking stream well lin'd with Willows and had some difficulty in discovering a fording place but our Guides calling out to some Indians who were on the opposite side they came and pointed out a suitable spot ≶ had the water been two inches deeper without the assistance of rafts we could not have cross'd, we succeeded however without wetting any thing, we saw the remains of a stone Barrier made by the natives for taking small Fish but at this season it is abandoned. We advanced one mile in descending the River and encamped. Course S.E. 6 and West 1 miles. . . . The hills here are richly covered with the Juniper Tree fortunately . . . or we should be but poorly for fire wood there being no worm wood [big sagebrush] and no dry Willows.*

The 1961 edition places Ogden on Willow Creek (due to his mention of willow-lined banks?), a small, seasonal stream to the south of Lower Klamath Lake. This is not a credible location from the standpoint of both (a) the journal's previous courses and distances, and (b) Ogden's graphic description of a large, deep "River." He was referring to Lost River, a few miles east of the Olene Gap. The brigade had entered well within Modoc territory.[11] After crossing the river, probably at Olene Ford, Ogden sent several trappers upstream while he and the main party descended it to the west (probably past the point where the Lost River passes through Olene Gap, a short gorge in the transverse fault block.) Some persons have speculated that Ogden's "stone Barrier" would have been the so-called Stone Bridge, a low-water ford formed by a partially submerged basalt ledge, but this location would be much too far to the south. Rock fish-weirs, built by the Modoc Indians to entrap "suckers," were once located at many places along the Lost River.[12]

DECEMBER *"21" [20]: . . . The two men who started yesterday to examine the upper part of the River arrived with two Beaver, they report they found one Beaver Lodge. . . , the River is not long it receiving its waters from a chain of Lakes some of them of a large size, from all accounts this country is covered with Lakes.*

DECEMBER *"22" [21]: . . . upwards of 100 Indians assembled round our Camp . . . [The Chiefs] agreed with the accounts we received from our trappers that for some distance abroad is one continued Chain of Lakes but no River and beyond it barren Plains covered with stones and destitute of water and Animals . . . it also appears that the main River which receives the waters of all these Lakes and Rivers we are now encamped on takes its rise near our encampment of the 11th [10th] Inst. [December] but we have a mountain to cross on account of the Snow . . . we must retrace our steps. . . . but it is now two [too] late to repent, it is however so far satisfactory that we have visited it . . . otherwise we as well as others would have remained in doubt regarding it . . . our reward has been two Beaver.*

DECEMBER *"23" [22]: I did not raise Camp. . . . one of the Chiefs of this River informed us that some distance in advance there was a small river in which there are Beaver, but having been forbid by our Guides as well as other Indians to inform us of this . . . he has volunteered to accompany us I shall not refuse the offer . . . Our guides are not aware of our having obtained this information.*

Maintaining his bivouac near the south bank of Lost River for three days, Ogden debated the wisdom of leaving Upper Klamath Lake for the inhospitable (and beaver-poor) steppe-lands of the Lost River drainage. His "two men" undoubtedly ascended the river to its source at Clear Lake and the adjacent marshes (now inundated by Clear Lake Reservoir). The "main River" of which Ogden somewhat wistfully writes would be the Klamath and, despite the deep snow through which the brigade would now have to return, he determined to "retrace" his steps. However, the next day's discussion with "one of the Chiefs" persuaded the chief trader, ever eager both to increase his beaver harvest and to expand his knowledge of new geography, to continue southward instead.[13]

December "24" [23]: we took a Southern Course over a barren Plain.

This northwestward view from the floor of Poe Valley (part of the "barren Plain") looks back over Ogden's previous route: the juniper-covered hills (left) between Poe Valley and Olene Gap, the dark hump of Moyina Hill (center-left) and the snow-covered hills (center-right) at the far (north) edge of Swan Lake Valley. (Photo by author)

DECEMBER *"24" [23]: At day light our Guides took their departure on their return home [to the Klamath villages] . . . At 10 A.M. we started . . .—we took a Southern Course over a barren Plain and advanced 10 miles and encamped. . . . the weather very foggy which prevented our seeing any distance in advance. Here we have certainly not an over abundance of water a sufficiency however for ourselves but none for our horses and there being no snow they must go without.*

Journeying south from Lost River on what he thought was Christmas Eve, Ogden most likely skirted the low range of hills along the west side of the Poe Valley and then crossed over them west of Buck Butte. The "barren Plain" of which he complained would be the flat terrain north of the historic shoreline of Tule Lake. The brigade probably camped about three or four miles northwest of Malin. The next day being, according to the chief trader's reckoning, Christmas Day, the group did not raise camp. Ogden fretted about their dwindling food supply (dogs purchased from the natives) but remarked positively about the improved weather.

DECEMBER *"26" [25]: . . . At nine A.M. we started and did not encamp untill 3 P.M. ≤ we travelled over a level Country well wooded with worm wood, this looks like Snake [River] Country, to the west of us we saw at some distance five Lakes, this certainly is a country of Lakes but not of Rivers or Beaver and the more I see of it the less opinion I have of it . . . a number of Huts of Indians were seen scattered in all directions over the plains. . . . We encamped on a small Brook, again not an over abundance of water. Our course South, dist. 15 miles. . . . Six Indians paid us a visit ≤ from their Blankets being made of Feathers of Ducks and Geese no doubt in the Fall*

December *"26" [25]: At nine A.M. we started . . . we travelled over a level Country well wooded with worm wood.*

This southward view toward Malin and Tule Lake shows the flat expanse of desolate country that greeted Ogden's eye on Christmas morning. (Photo by author)

December "26" [25]: One [mountain] in particular high above all others, pointed and covered with Snow—and from its height must be at a considerable distance from us.

This southwestward telephoto view of California's Mt. Shasta from near Malin, Oregon, provides approximately the same vantage point as Ogden had when he wrote his first and only mention of the 14,162-foot high peak. Irrigated cropland has replaced the formerly "worm wood"-covered "plains." (Photo by author)

and Spring there must be vast quantities in this quarter ≤ it cannot be otherwise there being so many Lakes and the country low altho on both sides of us the mountains are very high ≤ one in particular high above all others pointed and well covered with Snow—and from its height must be at a considerable distance from us. Our Guides inform'd us beyond these Mountains reside the Sastise a nation they are at present at war with.

Ogden trekked south-southeast, evidently staying well east of the Tule Lake shoreline, but close enough so that the scattered patches of open water in the tule-choked basin looked like "five Lakes" separated by marsh. The camp on the "small Brook" most likely was at one of the unamed, seasonal stream courses between Bloody Point and Horse Mountain. The expedition was now within the territory of the "Kokiwas" band of Modoc. The "Huts" Ogden mentioned may have been the villages of "Wuka" and "Welwa'sh," located just east of Tule Lake.[14] Modoc ethnography confirms the use of robes "woven of feather strips" during extreme winter temperatures.[15]

The mention of the high mountain, "pointed and well covered with Snow," is an unmistakable reference to the huge volcano presently called Mount Shasta. However, it must be stressed that although Ogden first mentioned the "Sastise" Indians at this time, he did not actually apply

16

December "28" [27]: following a chain of Lakes or more correctly one continued Lake.
This eastward view across Tule Lake Basin shows Ogden's southward (left-to-right) course along the far shore of Tule Lake. Copic Bay is situated just left of the dark butte in the center horizon. (Photo by author)

---

that name to the mountain in question, nor, I believe, did he *ever* use this term as a geographic name for the peak that now bears the name "Shasta." In short, Ogden failed to give this particular peak, visually prominent though it was, any name at all. The December "26" journal entry is the first—and the last—mention Ogden makes of the 14,000-foot high mountain.

DECEMBER "27" [26]: . . . *our two Guides refusing to proceed any farther with us caused us to be detained till 11 A.M. ere we started ≤ we however succeeded in making one of our Guides follow us but only for this day . . . it appears we are now as far as they know of the country . . . We started taking a South Course over truly a fine level Plain not a stick to be seen when we reached a small Lake and encamped ≤ so scarce was Wood that it was night ere the men found a sufficiency, some Roots were traded from the Natives.*

The brigade must have crossed a then-dry portion of Copic Bay (the "fine level Plain" without any wood) and encamped on the east side of the Copic Bay arm (the "small Lake") of Tule Lake, a nearly separate body of water that is connected to the main part of the Tule Lake basin by a narrow channel on the west. The Indians with whom Ogden's men traded for roots probably inhabited the nearby Modoc village of "E'uslis" (meaning "lake place") on the southeast shore of Tule Lake.[16]

DECEMBER *"28" [27]: At 9 A.M. we started taking nearly a South West Course following a chain of Lakes or more correctly one continued Lake until we reached the Mountains, here the Lakes in this direction appear to terminate, here we encamped . . . —in the forè part of the day and latter part we had a stony road ≲ the remainder fine and level—we saw a Camp of Indians in all Men and Women containing 60. . . . they had all Blankets made of Feathers . . . they are certainly entitled to some credit in devising such warm Coverings . . . the account the Indians give us of the advance Country in a South Direction being one continued Mountain and cut Rocks, [the brigade's hunters] attempted advancing but found it impracticable . . . the impediments must certainly be great hungry as they now are. . . . Dist. this day 12 miles.*

The 1961 edition puts the party in the vicinity of Mount Dome near "Sheep Dome" (Sheep Camp?) Lake. Again, this location tallies neither with the geographical descriptions for that day nor with the group's immediately preceding (and subsequent) travels in the area. Ogden must have begun the day by heading southwesterly, along the south edge of Copic Bay, and then turned west to skirt the south shore of the main part of Tule Lake, the "one continued Lake." His complaints about the "stony road" and the "cut Rocks" were justified; Ogden and his trappers crossed the northern edge of an immense lava field (now part of Lava Beds National

---

December "28" [27]: until we reached the Mountains, here the Lakes in this direction appear to terminate.

This southward view, taken from the now-drained basin of Tule Lake, shows Ogden's route along the shoreline (center) to near the base of Gillem Bluff (right). From there, the brigade headed southwest, some of its scouts ascending the snow-covered Medicine Lake Highlands (center-left horizon). (Photo by author)

Monument). That evening's camp would have been located near the east base of Gillem Bluff, at the southwest edge of the lake. This fifteen-mile long, north-south-trending fault block (which rises abruptly almost 1,000 vertical feet from the west shore of Tule Lake) would have been the "Mountains" at which the "Lakes . . . appear to terminate." The Indian camp Ogden described would almost certainly have been the large Modoc winter village of "Gu'mbat," situated near the southwest corner of Tule Lake.[17] The talk of "cut Rocks" to the south and west obviously worried the chief trader, lest he must finally backtrack the entire route to the Lost River crossing.

DECEMBER "29" [28] : Cold severe Lake froze . . . I sent [François] Payette on discovery in a Southern and two men in a South West Course to ascertain if we can pass and shall wait their arrival here . . . [The Indians] still persist in saying they know of no River in this quarter and altho we persist in making it appear we intend taking a Southern Course they warn us from the Cut Rocks Mountains and want of Water we cannot, being now as far advanced as we can go, but I must wait the return of my men ere I decide. Our five absent Hunters arrived . . . report they were obliged to leave their Horses it being impossible to pass owing to the cut Rocks. The men I sent

This northwestward view from the summit of Schonchin Butte (Lava Beds National Monument) shows Gillem Bluff (upper left quandrant of the photograph) and the former south shoreline of Tule Lake (center-right). In Ogden's day, the present mosaic of agricultural fields was the bed of the shallow, tule-choked lake. The northernmost tongue of the Devil's Homestead lava flow is visible as the dark area (center-left). (Photo by author)

on discovery also made their appearance one reports that following (Course) South with some difficulty but without endangering the lives of our Horses we may reach the end of the chain of Rocks, this is so far satisfactory and tomorrow we shall make the attempt. . . .

Even after weighing the gloomy geographic accounts of the Indians and the hardly less discouraging reports of his scouts, Ogden remained determined to press on across the Lava Beds.

DECEMBER *"30" [29]: This morning at an early hour our twelve Hunters started in quest of food and at nine A.M. we followed them leaving Indians and Guides, they still persisted in warning us we would starve and find no Beaver ≤ be it so we must give it a trial, we advanced ten miles ≤ road stony but not so bad as I expected altho to the right [west] of us it was certainly one continued chain of cut Rocks as far as the eye could reach nor does it appear to me we have done with them as we are now surrounded on all sides by high hills and mountains well covered with timber both Pine and Juniper. . . . Our Course South . . . we were however fortunate to find a Small Lake froze over but containing abundance of Water. In the evening the Hunters arrived without success and report from the top of the Mountains as far as they could see with the Glass [telescope] the Country for some distance in advance thick woods, and Plains covered with worm wood but not the least appearance of water or snow . . . and the mountains are far distant. This is a truly a gloomy account. . . . determined to advance but did not intend to do so without first examining the road and should send an advance [scout] to examine it.*

The brigade successfully skirted some of the most treacherous sections of the Lava Beds. The initially puzzling reference to the "continued chain of cut Rocks" as being on their *right*, or west, when the bulk of the lava field lay to the east, or left, of the southerly course, indicates that Ogden probably passed just east of the "Devil's Homestead," one of the most rugged and visually dramatic portions of the Lava Beds.[18] As for the location of the December "30" encampment, if the brigade's course turned from south to southwest after it had passed the southern foot of Gillem Bluff, then tiny Bonita Lake would be the obvious candidate for the "Small Lake froze over," especially since the approximate distance from Tule Lake also would agree with the mileage given by Ogden for this day's march. It is very doubtful, based on the distance and description given by Ogden, that the main group travelled as far south as Medicine Lake; however, it is likely that Ogden's hunters did head south and climb to one of the several volcanic summits of the Medicine Lake Highlands, and probably to the top of nearby Mt. Dome, north of Bonita Lake, as well.

DECEMBER *"31" [30]: Early this morning Mr. McKay with a man started to go in advance and should he not make his appearance tomorrow we may conclude he has met with success and proceed on ≤ I shall fell [feel] most anxious that he returns not.*

December "30" [29]: To the right [west] of us it was certainly one continued chain of cut Rocks as far as the eye could reach.

This view to the west, taken from somewhere very close to Ogden's path, shows the Devil's Homestead lava flow as it would have appeared during his trek southward from Tule Lake. Mt. Dome (center-right) rises just above the Gillem Bluff fault block. (Photo by author)

This wide-angle view from the summit of Schonchin Butte shows Gillem Bluff and Tule Lake (right), and Mt. Dome (left). The Schonchin lava flow is the nearest dark area; the Devil's Homestead lava flow is the dark line in the middle distance. Ogden's path skirted the eastern (lower) margin of the Devil's Homestead flow. (Photo by author)

"JANUARY 1, 1827" [Dec. 31, 1826]: The new year commenced with certainly a fine mild day altho the night was cold, the men paid me their respects. I gave them a dram [of rum or brandy] and 1 foot of Tobacco . . . As the Sun was on the eve of leaving us to my regret Mr. McKay arrived and confirms all the Natives informed us and farther that from the top of a mountain as far as he could see with the Glass it was one continued chain of mountains without the least appearance of water still less rivers and the road stony. . . . return we must and seek food where we can find it.

Ogden's "new year" did not begin auspiciously. McKay returned from his one-day reconnaissance, possibly to the summit of one of the cluster of peaks in the Medicine Lake Highlands due south of Bonita Lake, with bad news. The extensive lava fields and obsidian flows of the Medicine Lake area may have accounted for McKay's remarks about the "stony" road. The

December "30" [29]: We were however fortunate to find a Small Lake froze over but containing abundance of Water.

This northward view from the western margin of shallow Bonita Lake shows Mt. Dome on the horizon. Bonita Lake, the only water source Ogden found after leaving Tule Lake, marked his farthest advance to the southwest before returning to Tule Lake and Lost River. (Photo by author)

22

Wandering through the juniper-studded Lava Beds country, Ogden's men were unsuccessful as hunters of local mule deer (a trio of deer stand in front of the three tall trees near Gillem Bluff). (Photo by author)

---

rolling, upland terrain would not have provided any view of obvious river drainages to either the south or west—the directions in which Ogden had the most interest at this time.

The 1961 edition (p.49, n. 1) puts the brigade near Canby Cross (on the southwest side of Tule Lake) on this date. Tule Lake did, in fact, become known to Hudson's Bay Company trappers (and, hence, to later cartographers) as "New Year's Lake," almost certainly because of Ogden's passage along its shores around this date in 1827. However, it is plain from the journal entries given below that Ogden actually did not return to the shores of Tule Lake from his farthest southwest point of march (Bonita Lake?) until January "2" at the earliest.[19]

> JANUARY "2" [1]: *We made every preparation for starting ≦ Lodges down but it was near evening before our Horses were all found ≦ we were consequently obliged to remain, the scarcity of Grass is the cause of their going so far.*

> JANUARY "3" [2]: *. . . at sun sett twelve [horses] being found I started leaving four men to seek for the remainder and at midnight I overtook the Camp at the Indian Village seen on the 28th [27th, at southwest corner of Tule Lake] they had not been*

idle altho they considerably shortened our old track ≦ still it was night when they encamped. The Natives since we passed here have abandoned their Village but we could not discover what course they have taken . . . We took the liberty of demolishing their Huts for fire wood . . . —I should certainly regret that our side should cause a quarrel with these Indians, for so far their conduct toward us has been certainly most correct and orderly and worthy of imitation by all.

This particular entry is confusing. Did Ogden's use of "midnight" refer to that of January "2" [1] or to the following night? Whichever date was meant, the journal's mention of a shortcut indicates that the party probably skirted to the west of the Lava Beds and passed over the south end of Gillem Bluff in order to reach the "Indian Village" at the site of its December "29" encampment. On this date Ogden would indeed have been in the Canby Cross area. For the following three days he retraced his general route of December "24" through December "28" (although considerably shortening it in some portions) back to Lost River.

JANUARY "4" [3]: . . . *it was late ere we started from our Horses straying and advanced to our encampment of the 27th [26th; Copic Bay].*

JANUARY "5" [4]: *We started at an early hour . . . We left our old road and by taking a shorter route [along the edge of Tule Lake?] in the evening we reached our encampment of the 25th [24th; near Malin].*

JANUARY "6" [5]: *We again started at an early hour but wishing to follow down the River seen on the 24th [23rd; Lost River, which the brigade had last seen on that date] and not being sure of finding a fording place below we return'd to our old crossing place, here two Tents of Freemen separated from me taking our old road to the Lake [to Upper Klamath Lake] in hopes of either procuring Fish or Dogs. I followed down the Stream for ten miles when finding Mr. McKay with six of the Hunters we encamped. . . . what a fine River for Beaver nor can I account for it there is none.*

After recrossing the Lost River, several groups of "Freemen" (French-Canadian and Indian trappers not directly employed by the HBC) left the main party and retraced their late December route back to the Klamath villages. According to Ogden's journal entries for the first week in January, many of the Modocs they encountered were complaining of starvation as the local deer population was sparse; little wonder, then, that the chief trader permitted some of his men to return to the "Clammitte" village for badly-needed food supplies.

The 1961 edition compounds its original error here (p. 51, n. 1), when it claims that "Ogden's entry for 24 [23] December contains no reference to a river . . . [it is] assumed that Ogden here means Willow Creek which had he [sic] forded on 20 [19] December." As mentioned previously, Ogden actually would have first crossed the Lost River, not the shallow trickle of

Willow Creek, on December "20." He then camped on the south bank of the river for the next three days, until the morning of December "24" [23], when the party travelled south towards Tule Lake. Admittedly, the journal entry for that particular date does not refer specifically to a river (no doubt because Ogden had been camped next to it for the preceding four days), but his report for January "6" [5] does make sense when one remembers that the "24th" of December was the very day that he departed from Lost River. In other words, it was indeed the river that he had last seen on that date.

Ogden and the main party descended the Lost River for approximately ten miles, probably camping by the stream somewhere between Henley and Stukel. Here they remained for the next six days, hunting deer and bear while Payette and the other scouts reconnoitered the terrain to the west and south, probing for the best approach to the Klamath River.

JANUARY "9" [8]: . . . he [a trapper] also reports from what he could observe at a distance that he is of opinion we can reach the main River at its entrance into the mountains without going round the large Lake, this is contrary to what the Indians report and consequently . . . I must ascertain if this information can be relied on or not.

Unbeknownst to Ogden on the "6th" of January, the Klamath River (the "main River") lay less than ten miles west of their Lost River camp. The unnamed trapper must have climbed one of the low hills separating the two drainages and seen the "Clammitte" winding towards its passage through the Cascade Range. Ogden's native informants may have regarded the wide, marsh-lined stretch of the Klamath River below Klamath Falls to be uncrossable by the mounted brigade. The "mountains" would have been the series of 6,000-foot-high shield volcanoes of the southern Cascade Range, clearly visible directly to the west. The identity of the "large Lake" is slightly more problematical. It was probably Upper Klamath Lake (with which Ogden was already familiar), but possibly it was Lower Klamath Lake, which some of his scouts by then would have reached. The former is far more likely; Ogden definitely would have wished to avoid having to march around Upper Klamath Lake in order to reach the opposite side of the Klamath River (which, as he by then must have known, lay only a short distance west of his Lost River camp).

JANUARY "10" [9]: Early this morning I sent Payette & man to ascertain if it was possible to reach the River from this quarter, I also sent four men in different directions to trade all the provisions they possibly can so as to enable us if the Snow be not too deep to cross the Mountains [the Cascades].

JANUARY "11" [10]: . . . Payette arrived and informs me on account of Lakes and marshes we cannot reach the River and must now return to the Lake [Upper Klamath

*Lake] to procure a Guide. We have certainly a most circuitous route to make. . . .
We have now the lower part of the Clammit River to examine also represented by the
natives as abounding in Beaver . . .*

JANUARY *"12" [11]: I this morning sent men to the Freemen Tents [to notify those
trappers who had returned to the Upper Klamath Lake or Klamath Marsh villages] to
advertise them to raise Camp towards the Clammitt River as I purpose to reach that
quarter tomorrow.*

Curiously, even though Payette had returned with a discouraging report, the next day Ogden decided to reach the Klamath River directly
from his Lost River encampment. Perhaps he decided to gamble on the
correctness of the earlier trapper's account, and to trust that he could indeed reach the river's bank and cross to the other side. Ogden would
hardly have sent word to his absent "Freemen" to join him if he had intended to backtrack to Upper Klamath Lake.

Ogden's next journal entry is crucial; a correct geographic interpretation of the entire subsequent route depends upon where this point is
placed on the map.

JANUARY *"13" [12]: . . . I started and we had certainly cause to regret it ≦ the storm
increased as we advanced and the cold with it with our track being over a wide Plain
. . . [the storm] was increasing when we reached the River and had we been on foot I
am of opinion all were gone. The River here is a fine large Stream about 1/4 of a mile
in width deep and well lined with Willows taking as far as the eye can reach a Southern
Course ≦ within a short distance of this it discharges into a Lake ≦ this is certainly a
strange Country, in no direction can we possibly travel without seeing Lakes and all
connected together and I am of the opinion all discharge in this River ≦ but the natives
still persist in saying [the river] takes a bend to the Westward and passes through the
Mountains and we cannot cross there except in the summer season ≦ this may be
correct. . . . One of my trading party arrived with 16 Dogs.*

So, on a stormy, bitterly cold January "13," Ogden and his trappers
reached the Klamath River. But at what point did they actually reach it?
One local historian, the late Devere Helfrich of Klamath Falls, put the
brigade within the present city limits of Klamath Falls, near the bridge
aross the Link River—the narrow section of the Klamath River where it
first issues from Upper Klamath Lake.[20] The 1961 edition (p.52, n.1)
places the party at Beswick, near the Klamath (or Shovel Creek) Hot
Springs, California, nearly forty river-miles downstream. I believe both of
these interpretations to be incorrect.

Based on Ogden's uncharacteristically abundant geographic descriptions
for this date, it is evident that the brigade reached the "Clammitte" somewhere downstream of the narrow Link River section and upstream from
the marshlands of Lower Klamath Lake. The most probable location

*January "13" [12]: I started and we had certainly cause to
regret it ≤ the storm increased as we advanced and the cold
with it with our track being over a wide Plain [the storm] was
increasing when we reached the River.*

This southward view from a bluff overlooking the
Klamath River shows Ogden's course over the snow-
covered "wide Plain" (far left) to the river's edge (near the
U.S. Highway 97 bridge, visible at the lower left). (Photo
by author)

would have been the south end of "Lake Ewauna" (actually a slack, relatively wide section of the river immediately below Link River and downtown Klamath Falls), just upstream and across the river from the present
Weyerhaeuser mill. Formerly, the stretch of the Klamath just south of here
was considerably wider than at present, due largely to the natural im-
poundment of waters from Lower Klamath Lake just to the south.

The 1961 editors' reference to Beswick apparently stems from confusion
over Ogden's subsequent mention (on January "15") of nearby "Hot and
boiling Springs." Although they are now largely concealed by the urban
development of Klamath Falls, there were once several hot springs in the
immediate vicinity. Unless one were familiar with this fact (the springs are
not shown on most maps), it would seem logical to place Ogden at Bes-

wick (near Shovel Creek), the only hot springs within the wider area that are marked on recent maps.

What is the rationale for locating Ogden on the Klamath River, a short distance downstream from Klamath Falls? One must review Ogden's own words. The party's course of travel, which must have been generally westward, took them across "a wide Plain." This would have been the nearly flat terrain that separates the Lost River drainage from that of the Klamath River, between Henley and Texum. From the interpretation given in the 1961 edition, one could infer that this "wide Plain" might have been the Meiss Lake-Butte Valley area, but this would place Ogden much too far to

---

January "13" [12]: *The River here is a fine large Stream about 1/4 of a mile in width deep* [and] *taking as far as the Eye can reach a Southern Course within a short distance of this it discharges into a Lake.*

This westward view shows the Klamath River from very near the spot Ogden reached its banks on January "13." Four days later the brigade crossed, with the aid of canoes, to the opposite shore, near the present site of the Weyerhaeuser mill (right). The now-dry basin of Lower Klamath Lake is located to the south (left) of this view. (Photo by author)

the south. Ogden's description of the Klamath as a "fine large Stream about 1/4 of a mile in width" clearly eliminates both the Link River section and the Beswick section of the river, where the channel is considerably more restricted and nowhere approaches being a quarter-mile in width. This description would, however, apply to the Klamath near the Weyerhaeuser mill. Ogden's reference to the here-placid river as "taking as far as the eye can reach a Southern Course" also eliminates the Beswick section, where the river's downstream course through the steep terrain is quite definitely to the west. The section in the vicinity of the Weyerhaeuser plant flows south-to-southwest for several miles. Ogden quite plainly described a wide, relatively calm, southerly-flowing section of the Klamath River at a point *before* it enters the "mountains" (the Cascades); the Beswick section, in contrast, is a fairly narrow, turbulent, westward-flowing portion of the river that is situated well *within* the Cascade Range. The final clue in the January "13" journal entry is Ogden's mention of the river discharging "into a Lake." There is no lake west of Beswick (aside from two hydroelectric reservoirs, Copco Lake and Iron Gate Reservoir). Although the Link River section of the Klamath flows directly into "Lake Ewauna," this body of water is really only a widening of the river, and one that Ogden probably would not have considered a "lake." It is apparent that the "Lake" to which Ogden referred is actually Lower Klamath Lake, a once-vast basin of marsh and shallow, open water that lay adjacent to the river, no more than four miles south of Ogden's first Klamath River encampment.[21]

As mentioned previously, the importance of a correct identification of Ogden's Klamath River crossing point cannot be overstated. This location is the critical link upon which depends an accurate tracing of the brigade's entire subsequent route of travel through the Klamath and Rogue River basins. The Beswick location puts Ogden well downstream from what I believe was his actual crossing place, consequently skewing much too far to the west the inferred route of Ogden's northward march across the Siskiyou Mountains and into the Rogue River basin.

Ogden remained camped on the left (southeast) bank of the Klamath for three more days, awaiting the arrival of his absent "Freemen" and trading with the natives for a supply of dogs.

JANUARY "14" [13]: . . . two of the Freemen . . . rejoined us . . . We traded 1 Dogs this day. The natives paid us a visit to the number of eighty.

JANUARY "15" [14]: . . . Hot and boiling Springs are numerous in this quarter. N less than four within a short distance of our Camp and one in particular the wate boiling and it certainly appeared strange to me to see a small Insect, black enjoyin themselves swimming in this boiling water . . . None of these springs appear deep an the water when cold has not an unpleasant taste.

As Devere Helfrich has pointed out previously,[22] the geothermal spring of which Ogden specifically wrote is undoubtedly the "Devil's Teakettle," located in the present vicinity of the Klamath Union High School. Ogden and his trappers evidently occupied at least some of their time visiting the local "natural curiosities," such as the several hot springs located a relatively short distance northeast of their camp, within the present city limits of Klamath Falls.

JANUARY "16" [15]: *The two men who started on a trading excursion on the 10th [9th; those two Freemen who separated from the main party at Lost River crossing] rejoined us this day with 16 Dogs ≤ the remainder of the Freemen also made their appearance.*

By this time Ogden's men had become quite disgruntled with their poor returns. Beaver were scarce. Some of the men theatened to retrace their path north from the Klamath Marsh area to the Klamath-Deschutes divide, and then home to Fort Vancouver. However, the deep snows on the divide (the present Chemult-Crescent area on Highway 97) evidently persuaded them to cast their lot with the fortunes of their chief trader.

JANUARY "17" [16]: *Plots and plans occupied the greater part of the Freemen last night and this morning but on giving orders to cross the River I did not hear one voice to the contrary ≤ the Natives assisted us with two Canoes and towards evening we were all with our Horses safely landed on the Northside of the River. . . . [the Freemen] finding themselves thus situated I am of opinion will follow me to the Mountain [the Cascade Range, lying immediately to the west] but if farther I cannot say.*

Ogden had now crossed the Klamath River, probably at or slightly north of the Highway 97 bridge, just north of the present Weyerhaeuser mill. Although at first puzzling, his mention of the "North" side is understandable since the river here follows a generally southwest course. Once across the Klamath, the trappers again encamped for three full days. They traded with the nearby Klamath village on Link River for all the natives' remaining dogs while Ogden arranged for a guide to accompany the brigade downstream.[23]

SECTION TWO:
Klamath River Crossing to the Siskiyou Summit

THIS PORTION of Ogden's expedition brings him from the Klamath River crossing downstream in a generally westerly direction to the point where he turned north, away from the Klamath, and ascended the Siskiyou Mountains. Crossing the Siskiyous on February "9," the brigade entered the Rogue River drainage. As discussed earlier, this is, for the purposes of the commentary, the decisive section of Ogden's route. If the Klamath River crossing is one crucial point for the interpretation of the rest of Ogden's journey, the actual site of his "right turn" to the north (into the Rogue River drainage) is hardly less important.

Because it places Ogden at Beswick on January "13," the 1961 version of the route shows the brigade as following the Klamath downstream as far as Beaver Creek (near the present communities of Klamath River and Oak Knoll) and then ascending north up Beaver Creek to cross the Siskiyous into the headwaters of the Little Applegate River, crossing the mountains somewhere between Red Mountain and Siskiyou Peak.[24] This locates the group's summit crossing about ten air-miles too far to the west, in itself certainly not a large discrepancy. But in this geographic context, it is enough to place Ogden within the wrong drainage system of the Rogue River basin and, thereby, to "throw-off" his entire later path of travel. Using the 1961 interpretation, many of Ogden's distances, directions, and geographic descriptions for this and the following section simply do not coincide with the actual lay of the land. In some cases, the contrasts between word and reality are extreme. However, by placing his "Clammitte" River crossing a short distance below Klamath Falls (which agrees with his

31

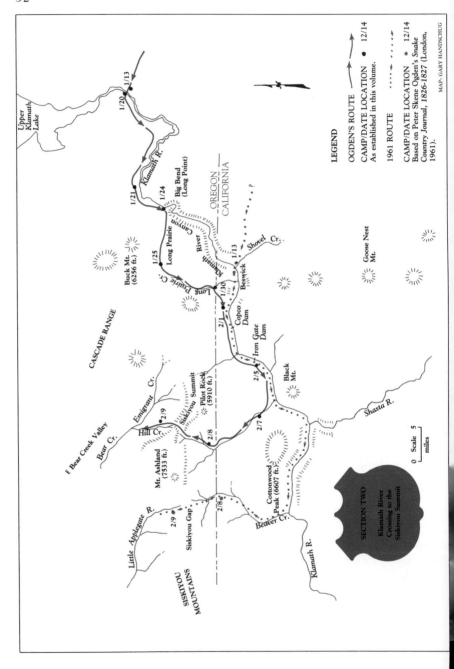

LEGEND

OGDEN'S ROUTE

CAMP/DATE LOCATION ● 12/14
As established in this volume.

1961 ROUTE

CAMP/DATE LOCATION ● 12/14
Based on Peter Skene Ogden's Snake
Country Journal, 1826-1827 (London,
1961).

MAP: GARY HANDSCHUG

Upper Klamath Lake

1/13
1/20
Klamath R.
1/21
1/24
Big Bend
(Long Point)
Canyon
River
Klamath
OREGON
CALIFORNIA
1/13
Shovel Cr.
Beswick
Goose Nest Mt.
Long Prairie
Long Prairie Cr.
1/30
Copco Dam
2/1
Iron Gate Dam
Buck Mt.
(6256 ft.)
1/25
CASCADE RANGE
2/5
Black Mt.
Pilot Rock
(5910 ft.)
Siskiyou Summit
2/8
2/7
Shasta R.
Emigrant Cr.
2/9
Hill Cr.
Mt. Ashland
(7533 ft.)
F Bear Creek Valley
Bear Cr.
Cottonwood
Peak (6607 ft.)
Beaver Cr.
Little Applegate R.
2/9
Siskiyou Gap
2/8
SISKIYOU
MOUNTAINS
Klamath R.

0 Scale 5
miles

SECTION TWO

Klamath River
Crossing to the
Siskiyou Summit

previous travels) *and* by locating his northward turn at Cottonwood Creek, one can follow the route of Ogden's journey quite closely, and with consistent agreement between his daily journal entries and the actual terrain he traversed.

In brief, after crossing the Klamath, the brigade followed the river down to the vicinity of Big Bend Canyon. There it left the river for several days by taking a westerly course across the "Pokegama Plateau" country (south of Oregon Highway 66), and then rejoined the Klamath at a point within the present Copco Lake Reservoir. Continuing downstream for about fifteen miles, the trappers turned north at the mouth of Cottonwood Creek, following that stream to its head at the crest of the Siskiyou Mountains, very near to the present summit crossing of Interstate 5.[25]

JANUARY "18" [17][1827]: *Fair weather but cold ≤ I wait here for my [Klamath] guide . . . cursed Country I not onely feel but am wretched and unhappy ≤ God grant we were all safe out of it and in a Country of Beaver.*

JANUARY "19" [18]: . . . . *late in the evening the Indian Chief with my Interpretor arrived ≤ they succeeded in procuring a Guide.*

JANUARY "20" [19]: *We made every preparation for starting but were again disappointed ≤ a violent storm of wind and rain which continued all day.*

Ogden's guide expressed reluctance to travel very far downstream because of fear of "enemies." These native foes proved to be the Shasta (whom Ogden called "Sastise"), who inhabited the Klamath River Canyon below Big Bend.

JANUARY "21" [20]: . . . *at Sun rise we started, Our Course South following the banks of the River for nine miles when the River taking a North West Course we continued following it for four miles and encamped, the road was most fatiguing for our Horses sinking in mire from the rain yesterday ≤ the Country level untill the last four miles when we had a hilly road well covered with Norway Pines also a few Oak Trees of a small size. The soil in general in this Country with little labour would produce well.*

Ogden's stated course and distance for this day would not match the Klamath River terrain below Beswick, where the river flows westward through a steep-walled canyon. Ogden paralleled the right bank of the Klamath downstream from near the Weyerhaeuser mill site for the approximately eight miles that it flows south-southwest. This is very flat terrain. From any of the low rises near this "nine miles" distance point (located back from the river itself), Ogden would have seen where the river makes a sharp bend to the northwest, and then would have adjusted his course accordingly. His abrupt, mid-day course change most likely occurred about two miles due east of the present town of Keno. "Four miles" or so of subsequesnt northwestward (and now "hilly") travel definitely would have brought him several miles downstream from (northwest of) Keno, between Oatman Lake and the mouth of Spencer Creek. Ogden's mention of "Norway Pines" (ponderosa pine) and "Oak Trees of a small size" (the scrub variety of Oregon white oak) matches the native vegetation of the Keno area. This is the first mention of "Norway Pines" that his journal contains for many days; ponderosa pine would have been nearly absent from his previous traverse of the Lost River drainage.

Camping west of present Keno for the next two days, Ogden sent out his hunters. They returned with badly needed meat—"Red Deer" (elk)—and with news of very deep snow in the "Mountains." These men probably advanced northwest into the Cascades, possibly penetrating as far as the upper Spencer Creek-Buck Lake area. In camp on January "22," Ogden remarked that "the Country before us [downstream, and to the west in general] appeared hilly and well wooded." Despite "the depth of Snow in the mountains from six to eight feet," he and his men were cheered by reports of plentiful game.

JANUARY "24" [23]: From the dense fog we did not find our Horses untill 11 A.M. when we started taking a South Course ≶ to avoid the rocky banks of the River and to shorten our distance we crossed over two points of land and encamped on the banks of the River ≶ here for some distance in advance and in our rear as far as we can see is one continued rapid fall & Cascade and our Guide informs us beyond this Salmon do not ascend ≶ so this is a convincing proof if I had any doubts that this River discharges in the Ocean, in this spot formerly a Tribe of Indians resided but have all been destroyed by the Clammett Nation . . . We had a woody and hilly road and our Horses altho not loaded had in many places hard labour to extricate themselves from the mire ≶ consequently our progress was slow and altho we were five hours marching we did not advance six miles ≶ we crossed over a small Fork which the Trappers examined and report not many years since was well stock'd in Beaver but at present not one remains.

Ogden followed the now south-southwest course of the Klamath, crossing Spencer Creek, undoubtedly the "small Fork which the Trappers [had previously] examined," "and reached the upper vicinity of what is called "Big Bend Canyon." About mid-way along this day's travel the now-turbulent Klamath begins to enter a very narrow gorge (leading into the present Big Bend-Long Point-Salt Caves area). This fact explains Ogden's reference to the river as "one continued rapid fall & Cascade," and it may also account for the chief trader's decision "to avoid the rocky banks" by crossing the level plateau above the edge of the gorge (by travelling west of Long Point) before descending again to the river. However, it is also possible (and I believe it to be somewhat more likely) that Ogden returned to the river just above Big Bend; a descent into the gorge below Big Bend would have been very hazardous (as Ogden's next journal entry makes abundantly clear).[26] In addition, this point is indeed the historic upper limit of most salmon runs on the Klamath River.[27] Ogden must have camped within a mile or two upstream (*or*, less likely, downstream) from Big Bend. The "Tribe of Indians" he mentioned probably were a band of Shasta.

JANUARY *"25" [24]: . . . started at an early hour leaving the River in our rear taking nearly a due West Course, on starting for four miles we had certainly a most hilly road and altho the remainder of our days journey was not hilly, it was far from being level ≤ the road being hard our Horses had good footing ≤ in the afternoon we reached a small Brook and Plain just in time as the rain commenced at the same time. . . . The Trappers made several attempts to reach the river but could not ≤ I also made an effort but in vain ≤ for upwards of ten miles perpindicular cut rocks not less than five hundred feet in height, on encamping I again sent men with Traps to examine the river, late in the evening they returned having found three Beaver Lodges in a small River, that the main River is as far as they could see is still one continued rapid. . . . In our travels this day I saw the White Pine of a very large size Ceedor also some Wild Plane Trees . . . from this place [just above Big Bend Canyon] to its sources [near Klamath Falls] the River is navigable for large Craft [canoes or bateaux] ≤ all the impediments can easily be overcome and with little labour . . . 12 miles.*

This is another clue-filled entry. Ogden left the Klamath turning "due West" for about a dozen miles. Why did he do this? The answer is apparent from his description of the river gorge: "perpindicular cut rocks not less than five hundred feet in height . . . the main River . . . still one continued rapid." This is an accurate (and for Ogden, a fairly vivid) description of the Klamath River's sheer-walled canyon below Big Bend; the 600-to 1,000-foot deep gorge extends for over six miles downstream. The cliffs that tower above either side of the Klamath are so precipitous that it is little wonder that Ogden and his trappers did not reach the river.

Twelve miles of westerly travel across "not hilly . . . [but] far from being level" country (probably over Hayden Mountain Pass) and through a forest containing "White Pine of a very large size [probably sugar pine], Ceedor [incense-cedar] also some Wild Plane Trees" would put Ogden's January "25–29" camp at or near Long Prairie, at the head of Long Prairie Creek (the "small Brook and Plain").[28] Thus the brigade traversed the rolling upland of what some local people call the "Pokegama Plateau." The travel that day must have closely paralleled the present route of Oregon Highway 66.

How does the 1961 edition trace Ogden's temporary departure from the Klamath? The relevant editorial comment (p. 57, n. 1) has him leaving the river at Camp Creek (within the present Iron Gate Reservoir, almost 30 miles below Big Bend) and travelling "cross-country" into the Cotton-

January "25" [24]: The Trappers made several attempts to reach the river but could not ≤ I also made an effort but in vain ≤ for upwards of ten miles perpindicular cut rocks not less than five hundred feet in height.

This southeastward view from Long Point shows the Klamath River's "Big Bend Canyon" as it must have appeared to Ogden. Dissuaded by the forbidding chasm from following the river, the brigade turned directly west from Long Point. (Photo by author)

wood Creek drainage near Hornbrook. This route would have Ogden leaving a relatively easy stretch of the river in order to traverse directly across a system of high-gradient streams (Camp Creek and Scotch Creek) and intervening ridges (which would have been *very* "hilly") to Cottonwood Creek. Additionally, the 1961 route fails to explain Ogden's striking description of the river gorge. Although the Klamath in the vicinity of Copco Lake-Iron Gate Reservoir does flow through a rather deep canyon, this canyon nowhere approaches being a gorge of "perpendicular cut rocks," over five hundred feet high. It is actually a wide "canyon" of relatively gentle slopes (twenty-five to thirty-five percent average) that are vegetated with grass, brush, scattered oaks and juniper. These slopes would have been easily descended by horses. In contrast, the Big Bend to Long Prairie route tallies quite well with virtually all of the chief trader's descriptions for that date.

Ogden remained camped at or near Long Prairie for four more days. His men fanned out into the surrounding area to hunt and trap.

January "26" [25]: We were roused from our Beds before day light from the heavy rain all night, the small brook . . . was this morning a large Stream and divided in many Streams.

Encamped at Long Prairie, shown here during the moist "runoff" season, Ogden awakened to find the formerly dry "Plain" to be a rain-soaked morass. (Photo by author)

JANUARY "26" [25]: *We were roused from our Beds before day light from the heavy rain all night, the small brook . . . was this morning a large Stream and divided in many Streams . . . the Country before us is covered with water. . . . My Guide having informed me that the tribe of Indians we are to see are not far off I sent him and my interpreter to discouver them and to warn them of our being near at hand and that we were peacibly inclined towards them . . . as our present Guide already appears nearly as great a stranger in this quarter as we are in this Country of Mountains and hills.*

JANUARY "28" [27]: *. . . strange Climate yesterday we had a fine warm sunny day and now we have truly a winter day. . . . My interpreter with two Indians made their appearance ≦ stout men and well clad their Language differs but little with the Clammitts. . . . it is to be regretted this Country has been allowed to remain so long unexplored altho certainly our Establishments are not far distant from it . . . but why go far in quest of Beaver when the Williamette afforded a sufficiency.*

JANUARY "29" [28]: *Late last night one of the Trappers arrived and . . . informed he had found seven Beaver Lodges ≦ this was certainly most agreeable news . . . were it not for the Deer kill'd yesterday I should have attempted raising Camp.*

The numerous meadows (what the early American settlers termed "prairies") of this relatively flat part of the Cascade Range are notoriously poorly drained. A downpour of rain will often temporarily turn places such as Long Prairie into shallow ponds. When wet, the volcanic clay soils become extremely sticky, adhering in great clumps to the feet of man and horse alike. This may account for Ogden's comment on January "27" that "from the present state of the roads we did not attempt raising Camp."[29]

JANUARY "30" [29]: *We had Snow during the night . . . I rais'd Camp ≦ we advanced onely eight miles and had a most wretched road our Horses wading in water and mire . . . but we are in a strange Country and amongst strange Indians whose intentions towards us we have yet to learn . . . We had a woody track Norway Pine and Cedar and in a small Plain which we crossed I was suprised to see a flock of Quails the first I have seen since my residence in the Indian Country . . . one of the Trappers arrived with nine Beavers ≦ a glorious sight to me . . . we are now encamped on a small brook and at some distance from the main stream [the Klamath]. Course South West.*

The birds likely were a flock of mountain quail, the largest of North American quail. Ogden advanced generally southward, towards the Klamath River, for less than ten miles. He probably travelled down Long Prairie Creek (the "small brook") and stopped less than four miles north of the Klamath. There he remained camped through the next day's snow storm while his trappers explored the nearby Klamath for beaver sign.[30]

January "30" [29]: we advanced onely eight miles and had a most wretched road. . . . We had a woody track Norway Pine and Cedar. . . . we are now encamped on a small brook.

Travelling south along Long Prairie Creek, shown here about eight miles from the brigade's previous camp, the horses had great difficulty negotiating the wet, slippery clay soils of the Pokegema Plateau's pine forest. Ogden's January "30" camp was somewhere near this spot. (Photo by author)

JANUARY "31" [30]: *The violence of the Snow Storm prevented us even from leaving our Lodges. . . . [later that day he wrote:] We now remain onely five men in the Camp. . . . the Trappers . . . report most favorably of the River ≦ altho the current is strong and Rapids numerous ≦ still in every eddy they have seen there is appearance of Beaver . . . —tomorrow we shall if the weather permits bend our Course towards the River and the remainder of our Traps shall be in motion.*

*February "1" [Jan. 31]: we started taking a due West Course
and at 5 P.M. we reached the River altho the distance was not
more than five miles but the road was most wretched. . . . the
Horses . . . sinking knee deep in mire.*

Still plagued by the sticky volcanic soils, Ogden descended from the edge of the Pokegema Plateau (right) via
Spannus or Raymond Gulch (just right of center) to the
Klamath River (here flooded beneath the waters of Copco
Lake reservoir). This view looks downstream (northwest)
toward the point where Ogden rejoined the Klamath after
his week-long detour around Big Bend Canyon. (Photo by
author)

FEBRUARY "1" [Jan. 31]: *It was 11 A.M. ere our Horses were found when we started
taking a due West Course and at 5 P.M. we reached the River altho the distance was
not more than five miles ≲ but the road was most wretched ≲ independent of stones
and Hills the Horses from the time they started until we reached the River were sinking knee deep in mire . . . here we are surrounded by oaks, soft Maple and Grass six
inches long and green as in the summer . . . the banks of the river here are certainly
high and the river not only deep but wide current strong and whirlpools numerous a
number of small streams discharge into it the greater part have been examined [by
Ogden's trappers during the previous day] but from their rapid descent destitute of
Beaver, the Country around us is certainly most hilly ≲ to the South West of us lofty
rocky Mountains equal in height from the distance I could see them to any I have yet
seen and they appear to have many branches ≲ they certainly have a bold appearance
≲ we must hope that we have not them also to cross in the Winter season . . . As
soo[n] as we were encamped yesterday I accompanied my Guide and Indian Chief to
an Indian Hut.[31] . . . their sole support appears to be Acorns ≲ of these they have a
large stock and altho subsisting entirely on them they were well in flesh.*

On "February 1" (actually the final day of January), Ogden travelled a
relatively short distance west from his previous camp and reached the
Klamath River via Spannus Gulch or Raymond Gulch (at a point now
beneath Copco Lake, a place aptly called "Beaver Basin" by later residents). The Klamath makes a short turn to the northwest below Long
Prairie Creek, so a westward course from his campsite would indeed have

---

February "1" [Jan. 31]: here we are surrounded by oaks,
soft Maple and Grass six inches long and green as in the
summer.

The lush oak woodland along this stretch of the
Klamath River (shown here at Beaver Basin) came in for
special mention in the chief trader's journal. The brigade
spent five days trapping in this vicinity before continuing
downriver to the west. (Photo by author)

brought Ogden to the river. Spannus Gulch, said to have been the route of a major Indian trail by local old-timers, was Ogden's most probable path to the river. The Klamath here flows through a fairly wide canyon, an open savanna with scattered oaks. The Klamath River, although still rough in many places, is a much calmer stream at this point than it is upstream in the gorge between Big Bend and Beswick.

As the brigade reached the southern edge of the heavily forested Poke-gama Plateau and began its descent down the lightly wooded slopes to the river, Odgen had a clear view of the jumbled mass of "lofty rocky Moun-tains" to the southwest. These were the Scott and Salmon Mountain ranges, which, together with the Siskiyous, comprise the bulk of the "Klamath Mountain Province" of southwest Oregon and northwest Cali-fornia. The nearest of these peaks were between twenty and thirty miles southwest of Ogden's viewpoint, but more distant ridges and peaks would also have been visible. So far as can be determined, Peter Ogden would have been the first Euro-American land-based explorer to see and com-ment on these mountain ranges.

At this point, the reader may well be wondering why Ogden's journal entry for this date contained no reference to the volcanic peak now called Mount Shasta. Could he have actually lumped it in with his description of the Scott-Salmon ranges to the southwest? This is very doubtful, both be-cause of Ogden's use of the term "many *branches*" (certainly an apt charac-terization of the Klamath Mountains, but not of Shasta) and, more impor-tantly, because Mount Shasta is situated slightly *east*-of-south from Og-den's "February 1" vantage point.

How could he have failed to see and again report the presence of this huge, 14,162-foot high volcanic peak? (Remember that he *had* noted it over a month previously, when the brigade was in the Tule Lake area.) The facts of local geography can solve the riddle of this seemingly inex-plicable omission: Ogden's view of Mount Shasta simply was blocked by the intervening chain of volcanic mountains, known today as the Goose-nest Range. The summit of Shasta lay over forty miles south-southeast from Ogden's location. His viewpoint on the rim of the Klamath River canyon was situated at an elevation of less than 3,900 feet. The Goosenest Range is a twenty-five-mile long, north-south-trending line of shield vol-canoes that intervenes directly on the line-of-sight between Ogden's prob-able location and Mount Shasta; four of the peaks are between 7,000 and 8,000 feet in elevation. No large mountain was visible from this low van-tage point, hence no mountain was mentioned in that day's journal entry. From Beaver Basin westward to Cottonwood Creek, Ogden's route fol-lowed the bottom of the Klamath River canyon, where the view south to-wards Mount Shasta would have been blocked by the 1,000-foot high can-yon slopes that rise directly from the river bank. Later, although Mount

Shasta is visible from many places in the upper Cottonwood Creek Valley, Ogden still failed to mention it in his reports for those dates. Weather conditions may have continued to obscure it from Ogden's view during those two days, or perhaps he saw the peak but neglected to comment on it. Why? Possibly merely because he had already noted its existence before. Also, by that time, Ogden's attention would have been directed north, towards the Siskiyou Mountains he was about to cross, and the reportedly beaver-rich river that lay beyond them. Ogden remained camped near Beaver Basin for three full days. His trappers, eager to gather prime pelts, scattered along the river and its tributaries.

FEBRUARY "2" [1]: . . . the Trappers . . . since gone up a Fork and from their non appearance supposes they have found Beaver ≤ the Natives not numerous and peacibly inclined, two of our Hunters who have been for the last six days on the Mountains also made their appearance well loaded with Meat. . . . altho the River is well stock'd in Wood of different kinds they [beaver] do not appear to relish it but subsist entirely on Roots and Grass . . . their favourite food is the Aspines Poplar and Willows and of these I see none in this quarter ≤ still the upper part of the River as well as the large Fork we examined were all well lin'd with Willows water deep and without rapids still without Beaver[32] ≤ here again it is the reverse for so far as we have examined almost one continued rapid and current very strong and we have Beaver.

FEBRUARY "4" [3]: . . . this spot is now nearly clear of Beaver and I onely wait the arrival of Mr. McKay [whom Ogden had sent upstream to ascertain the number of beaver] for his news which will enable us to raise Camp. . . . In the evening Mr. McKay arrived with 6 Beavers ≤ the report of the success of our two Trappers in the rear [upstream, possibly near Beswick] was certainly an exageration ≤ we had also a visit from two of our Trappers who came with 6 Beavers and report as follows, [Ogden paraphrases:] [″]we followed down the stream a considerable distance when our progress was arrested by the rocky Mountains the River taking its course through them at the foot of the mountains we saw a Camp of Indians . . . [the Indians] gave them [the trappers] to understand that in the direction they were then in they [the trappers] could not from the cut Rocks cross the Mountains but there was a road pointing to the Eastward[″] ≤ he also added to the above [″]you will on the other side find Br.[beaver] more numerous than here,[″] ten men have started to find a crossing place

During this three-day respite, Ogden's trappers apparently divided into small groups and explored many of the local streams. Two of them ventured quite some distance downriver. From their account, which Ogden recorded in his journal, these men undoubtedly descended past the mouth of Cottonwood Creek, putting them about twenty miles below the party's main camp, at the point where the river begins its tortuous westward course through the steep terrain of the Siskiyou Mountains' portion of the rugged "Klamath Mountain Province." They would have followed the

Klamath at least to the west side of Black Mountain, and may have neared the mouth of the Shasta River, which flows from the flanks of Mt. Shasta northwards to the Klamath. The "Camp of Indians" that they visited most likely was the Shasta village several miles below the mouth of Cottonwood Creek. There they learned that it would be very difficult to "cross the Mountains" (to the north?) from anywhere downstream, but were told of a "road pointing to the Eastward" that would lead them to a beaver-rich country. Because of the brigade's subsequent travels, it is apparent that the Shasta were speaking of the Rogue River drainage, immediately to the north.

Why does Ogden write "road pointing to the Eastward" when the trail over the Siskiyous actually was a northerly route? One possible explana-tion, of course, is the fact that Ogden was reporting on a "second-hand" conversation, one that may well have been garbled through miscommuni-cation between the trappers and the Indians. ("Eastward" travel would have had the brigade turn around and ascend the Klamath.) In addition, the location of the Shasta camp "at the foot of the Mountains" (down-stream from Cottonwood Creek and within the Siskiyou Mountains) would have put the two trappers west of the trail that led north up the Cottonwood Valley and over the Siskiyous. At any rate, later journal en-tries make it clear that the Shasta Indians certainly would have been refer-ring to the Bear Creek-Rogue River Valley across the Siskiyou Mountains.

FEBRUARY "5" [4]: We rais'd our Traps . . . we however proceeded on untill we reached a small brook and encamped nearly at its discharge in the main Stream [the Klamath]—all the Trappers in our rear are to raise their Traps and join us tomorrow . . . from the time we started untill we encamped a most hilly road and also one third of the distance very stony ≤ we followed the banks of the River and all along one continued Rapid and Cascade ≤ it is indeed suprising that Beaver should inhabit such rough water . . .—as far as we can see before us the Country is still very hilly and bare of wood altho along the banks of the River Oaks are numerous, Soil this day of a redish colour more the appearance of clay than soil. Distance 12 miles ≤ Course South West.

The "small brook" was probably Brush Creek, just downstream from Iron Gate Dam. Here Ogden camped through the following day while a group of ten trappers evidently reconnoitered the area below the mouth of Cottonwood Creek. Ogden also acquired new Indian guides, Shastas, who knew the "roads in the Mountains." The "most hilly road" must mean that Ogden travelled parallel to, and just above, the Klamath, across the open, south-aspect slopes of the canyon. The numerous outcrops of volcanic tuff clays that are exposed between Beaver Basin and Brush Creek (several have a definite scarlet hue) would account for Ogden's comment about the "redish colour . . . clay."

February "5" [4]: we followed the banks of the River and all along one continued Rapid and Cascade. . . . as far as we can see before us the Country is still very hilly and bare of wood altho along the banks of the River Oaks are numerous.

Ogden's route along the Klamath's "one continued Rapid and Cascade" now lies concealed deep beneath the waters of Copco Lake (shown here near Beaver Basin). He passed generally west along the foot of the bare, south-aspect slope of the river canyon (right) for nearly three days before turning north up Cottonwood Creek. Pilot Rock, visible here to the northwest (at center horizon), marks the drainage divide between the Klamath River and, to the north, the Rogue River. Ogden crossed the Siskiyou Summit into the Rogue drainage a short distance beyond Pilot Rock—one of several major landmarks unmentioned in his journal. (Photo by author)

FEBRUARY *"6" [5]: I had a long conversation with the strangers [the two new guides] and they with all the others I have seen are of the same opinion that on the other side of the Mountains we will find Beaver but that the Country is level only for a short distance when we will again have another Mountain to cross and as far as their knowledge extends it is one continued Mountain and altho strange as it may appear they know nothing nor ever heard any one make mention of the Sea . . . a convincing proof in the Salmon season the Salmon ascend this Stream, at events I am of opinion the Sea is far distant. . . .*

Note that the Indians spoke of the "other side of the Mountains" as being "level only for a short distance," when it then becomes "one continued Mountain." How "short" was a "short distance" to Ogden's native informants? Based on his subsequent travel route, the "level . . . Country"

February "7" [6]: following the main stream [Klamath River] untill 3 p.m. when we reached a large Fork . . . we ascended the Fork West North West.

This eastward view, from Interstate 5 to the Klamath, River looks directly upstream. Ogden followed the river down out of its upper canyon (upper-center) and into the small valley at the mouth of Cottonwood Creek (lower-center). The brigade then turned north and travelled along the banks of Cottonwood Creek (horizontal line of trees in the center-left of the photograph). (Photo by author)

---

they described almost certainly was the Bear Creek-Rogue River Valley. The "level" portion of this valley extends for about twenty miles northwest-southeast, and ends abruptly at the north amongst an extensive range of mountains. The two Klamath River Shastas probably would not have been personally familiar with the region north of this valley, hence their reference to "one continued Mountain." The local natives' ignorance of the Pacific Ocean, whether feigned or real, perplexed Ogden on several occasions.

On this date, ten trappers led by François Payette left Ogden's main group to continue descending the Klamath. It is clear from Ogden's later entries that the two parties agreed to rendezvous on the north side of the Siskiyous.

FEBRUARY "7" [6]: *Rain all night ≤ at an early hour this morning I sent off twelve Men with 20 Horses well loaded with Traps with an Indian to guide them across the Mountains ≤ we also started shortly after following the main stream untill 3 PM when we reached a large Fork which we ascended some distance and encamped just in time,*

This view of Cottonwood Creek (in the vicinity of Hornbrook, California) shows the snowy barrier of the Siskiyou Mountains to the north of Ogden's February "7" encampment. Mt. Ashland is near the center of the skyline. (Photo by author)

as the rain commenced shortly after, we had again this day a most hilly road and a muddy one—no appearance of snow in this quarter nor does there appear to be any great depth on the Mountains . . . they [Indians] are in a starving state subsisting entirely on Acorns ≤ we saw a number of Huts this day with all their little property in them. . . . From the time of our starting to our leaving the main Stream [the Klamath] it was still one continued Rapid and from the Mountainous Country it still continues the same altho it is navigable for craft ≤ many small streams discharge into it on both sides of the River it has not increased in size but has I suppose its depth ≤ with the exception of the different Forks that are well wooded, wood is rather scarce

Soil apparently rich and not stony. . . . Our Course untill we left the River South West and we ascended the Fork West North West. Distance this day 12 Miles.

This is another extremely critical point for correct interpretation of Ogden's itinerary. By inference, the 1961 edition puts the group's north-

---

February "8" [7]: Those [mountains] before us do not appear very high but we have been gradually ascending all this day and we are now encamped on high land which no doubt is the cause of their appearing low—in many parts wood appears scarce and in other parts abundant Oaks and Pine.

This northward view from upper Cottonwood Creek Valley shows "Siskiyou Summit" (the notch in the skyline, left-center). The surrounding hillsides are, as in Ogden's day, lightly forested with Oregon white oak and ponderosa pine. (Photo by author)

This southeastward view of the Cottonwood Creek Valley
(taken from the Mt. Ashland access road, about two miles
west of Siskiyou Summit) shows the area of Ogden's
travels between February "7" and "9." Mt. Shasta (center
horizon) is shrouded in clouds, much as it may have been
during Ogden's visit; Pilot Rock is on the far-left skyline.
(Photo by author)

ward course (after turning away from the river) up Beaver Creek, approximately twenty miles below the mouth of Cottonwood Creek. For a number
of reasons (many of them discussed previously), this is a very unlikely location for Ogden's departure north from the Klamath River. The river's
course for the ten miles above Beaver Creek is distinctly northwest, not
southwest. Additionally, the observation that "wood is rather scarce Soil
apparently rich and not stony" would hardly apply to the rocky, forested
slopes of lower Beaver Creek and the nearby river canyon.

Ogden descended along the north bank of the Klamath (still something
of a whitewater river along this stretch) to the mouth of Cottonwood
Creek, the "large Fork" that the brigade "ascended some distance." The
nearly continuous rains of the past two days had turned the volcanic soil
into a sticky morass, prompting the chief trader's complaints of the muddy
road. Relying on this figure of twelve miles of travel, Ogden's camp this

February "9" [8]: At 2 P.M. we succeeded in crossing the mountain with . . . less labour than expected ≤ the greatest depth of snow did not exceed more than a foot.

This northeastward view from the crest of Siskiyou Summit (taken in February) shows the brigade's route down the Hill Creek drainage into the Bear Creek Valley. (Photo by author)

day would have been along lower Cottonwood Creek, north of Horn-brook. This portion of the stream does flow from northwest to southeast, explaining Odgen's course direction of "West North West." The native "Huts" likely were the lodges of two Shasta villages near the mouth of Cottonwood Creek and near Hornbrook.[33]

Ogden was cautiously optimistic about the seemingly low depths of snow "in the Mountains." Ascending Cottonwood Creek, he would have clearly seen the barrier of the Siskiyou Mountains' "summit" astride his path, extending from 7,500-foot Mount Ashland on the left (west) to 5,900-foot Pilot Rock on the right (east). The pass lay between these two features.

FEBRUARY "8" [7]: . . . *we have now 30 men in advance with Traps in three different partys so by this plan no Stream will escape observation ≦ at eight we started and followed the Fork to its sources when we encamped we had truly a villainous road ≦ not onely hilly but muddy so much so that after the Horses were unloaded they were to be seen laying in all directions . . . we are now in the Mountains and tomorro I trust we shall leave them in our rear. . . . —the Country around us presents a gloomy and barren prospect ≦ Mountains covered with Snow of an extraordinary height ≦ those before us do not appear very high but we have been gradually ascending all this day*

Seen here in early spring, the crest of Siskiyou Summit (foreground) is bare of snow. Ogden's party ascended from the left and descended to the right, into the Bear Creek Valley of the Rogue River drainage. The site is now the junction of Colestein Road (Old Pacific Highway) and the Mt. Ashland access road; the "high hill" Ogden climbed to scout the new country most likely was the forested ridge seen in this photograph. (Photo by author)

This westward view shows Siskiyou *Gap* (center-right), the rugged pass between the Klamath River drainage and the Little Applegate River watershed that, according to the "1961 route," Ogden would have crossed on February "9." Approximately 5,900 feet above sea level (in contrast to Siskiyou Summit's 4,400-foot elevation), Siskiyou Gap retains abundant evidence of its characteristically deep winter snowpack in this late June photograph. Ogden's actual crossing point, Siskiyou Summit, is some ten miles east of here. (Photo by author)

and we are now encamped on high land which no doubt is the cause of their appearing low—in many parts wood appears scarce and in other parts abundant Oaks and Pine. Distance this day 10 miles ≦ Course West North W. Our Guide informs us in crossing the Mountains we shall see the Main Stream ≦ if so it must make a considerable bend but this I can scarcely credit for such a large body of water must take direct course to the Ocean.

Still vexed by the sticky clay soils of the Cottonwood Creek Valley, Ogden ascended the creek to an encampment a short distance above the mouth of Spaulding Creek (about two or three miles above Hilt, California). The party had just recrossed the 42nd Parallel, what is now the California-Oregon boundary, and had entered the rolling, oak- and pine-studded foothills south of the "Siskiyou Summit."[34]

FEBRUARY "9" *[8]: With the sun we were in motion and at 8 A.M. we started and at 2 P.M. we succeeded in crossing the mountain with grater [greater] facility and less labour than expected ≦ the greatest depth of snow did not exceed more than a foot if we found the ascend gradual the descent was certainly the reverse for in some parts so very steep it was with difficulty the Horses were prevented from falling with their loads ≤ all however reached this [the north] side, in safety . . . but probably Payette and party in the direction they have cross'd have not been so successfull where they cross'd it certainly has a stony and rocky appearance.*[35] *Following a small Stream for three miles I encamped ≤ all here looks like summer ≤ grass green and four inches in length and from the size of the wood the Oak here being nearly double the size of any I have seen this season induces me to suppose the Climate is milder. Altho I ascended a high hill I could not discover the Main Stream and concluded it is far distant. Shortly after we were encamped an Indian came boldly to my Tent and presented me with two fresh Salmon. . . . Course W N West.*

On February "9," Peter Odgen and his remaining men crossed the divide of the Siskiyou Mountains into the Rogue River drainage. The snowpack proved to be a very slight problem, and the trappers pressed on for an additional three miles north of the summit. (The advance parties probably had crossed over the pass on the previous day.) They entered an area of large oaks and lush grass.

The 1961 edition (p.69, n.1) puts the crossing site at or near a place called Siskiyou Gap (elev. 5,880 feet), about ten miles west of the 4,400-foot Siskiyou Summit (also called "Siskiyou Pass") that connects the Cottonwood Creek and Bear Creek valleys. Ogden's subsequent route is described as a descent of the Little Applegate River from its headwaters at Siskiyou Gap to its confluence with the main Applegate River. This crossing site is very unlikely, due not only to the brigade's previous itinerary, but also based on a review of the observations that Ogden recorded for this particular date. Siskiyou Gap, at nearly 6,000 feet, is a "subalpine" environment that is vegetated with mountain hemlock and Shasta red fir. It would be a very rare winter when the early February snowpack at this summit did not exceed several feet, especially during a winter as wet and cold as the 1826–27 season that Ogden documented. Further, the northward route up to the Klamath side of the Gap would have required ascent of extremely steep (50–60 percent) slopes, hardly a "gradual" climb. Finally, a trek of three miles down the Little Applegate River from Siskiyou Gap would place the brigade at an elevation of about 4,000 feet above sea level, in a narrow canyon that is very heavily forested with Douglas-fir, white fir, incense-cedar, and various pines. This dense conifer forest extends for at least an additional six miles downstream (well below the mouth of Glade Creek) before the first substantial groves of oak or grassy meadows begin to appear. It is very doubtful that Ogden's Shasta guides would have chosen such an inhospitable route; they must have followed the familiar foot-trail that linked the Klamath River and the Bear Creek Valley bands of the Shasta Indians.

54

February "9" [8]: Following a small Stream for three miles I encamped ≦ all here looks like summer . . . the Oaks here being nearly double the size of any I have seen this season.

The open oak woodland along Hill Creek, shown here about three miles north of Siskiyou Summit, came in for special mention by Ogden. Scenes like this no doubt reminded the chief trader of the country around Fort Vancouver and the lower Willamette Valley. The brigade camped somewhere very near this spot (located next to the Old Pacific Highway), among the large California black oaks and ponderosa pines. (Photo by author)

Ogden's route across the Siskiyous almost certainly paralleled the East Fork of Cottonwood Creek to its head (north, along the same general route as the subsequent California-Oregon Stage Road and the later Pacific Highway). Snow depths on the 4,400-foot Siskiyou Summit can vary considerably from winter to winter, but an average February snowpack would be about one foot. After reaching the crest, Ogden took a "W N West" course for three miles. The initial portion of this traverse was "very steep," but he soon descended to an area of oaks "nearly double the size of any" he had seen that season (probably California black oak) and green grass "four inches in length." Ogden clearly had descended the Siskiyou divide into upper Hill Creek, one of the southernmost tributaries of the Bear Creek drainage. The Hill Creek drainage flows north-northwest and provides the most direct access to the floor of the Bear Creek Valley near Ashland.[36] Ogden conceivably could have taken Carter Creek, which flows north-northeast from its head just east of Siskiyou Summit, but this route would have delivered him to the valley floor at a point somewhat too far south to agree with his later itinerary. Not only does Carter Creek flow in the wrong direction, but Hill Creek was the most likely route of the major north-south "Indian trail" used by Ogden's guides.

Ogden's camp this day was probably located along lower Hill Creek (near the ca. 1859 Major Hugh Barron house located next to old Highway 99). Situated at an elevation well below 2,900 feet, this is an area of oak woodland. With most of his trappers in advance, Ogden was ready to proceed northwest through the Bear Creek Valley to the Rogue River.

SECTION THREE:
Siskiyou Summit to the
Upper Rogue River

SECTION THREE of the journey brought Ogden from his Siskiyou Mountain crossing point northwest through the Bear Creek Valley (closely paralleling the present route of Interstate 5) to the Rogue River. The expedition ascended the left (east) bank of the Rogue northward to the vicinity of Trail Creek (although some of the trappers probably continued upstream at least to the Prospect area) and then retraced its steps to the confluence of Bear Creek and the Rogue River before continuing downriver. During their brief sojourn in the upper Rogue River basin, Ogden's trappers would have explored most of the major tributaries between Bear Creek and the forks of the Rogue.

The 1961 edition has Ogden descending the northwest-flowing Little Applegate River and the main Applegate River during this period, despite many contradictions between this route and the information given by Ogden. Although the surviving copy of the 1826–27 journal undoubtedly contains occasional copy errors (for example, wrong course directions) and even mistakes originally made by Ogden himself, it seems unlikely that the written record would be so at variance with the actual terrain as the 1961 version of the route would indicate. By following the brigade through the Bear Creek Valley, instead of the Applegate Valley, there is, as in the preceding sections, substantial agreement between Ogden's testimony and the facts of local geography.

The chief trader recorded a glowing description of the Bear Creek Valley countryside during the second week of February. Travelling near or through the future sites of Ashland, Talent, Phoenix, Medford, and Cen-

58

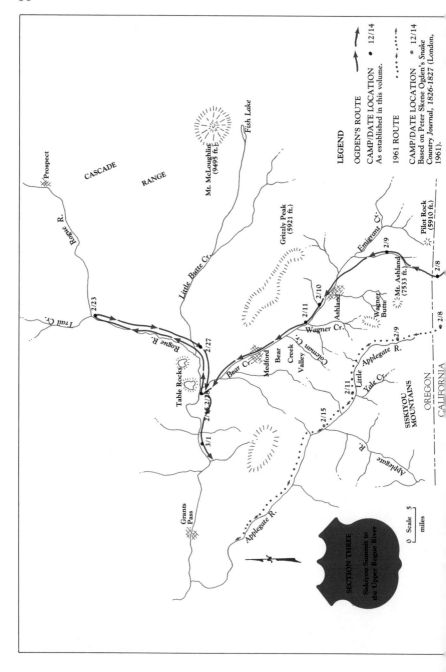

LEGEND

OGDEN'S ROUTE

CAMP/DATE LOCATION   ● 12/14
As established in this volume.

1961 ROUTE   ·····

CAMP/DATE LOCATION   ● 12/14
Based on Peter Skene Ogden's Snake
Country Journal, 1826-1827 (London,
1961).

Prospect

CASCADE

RANGE

Rogue R.

Trail Cr.

2/23

2/27

Table Rocks

Rogue R.

2/16 2/18

3/1

Grants
Pass

Applegate R.

Little Butte Cr.

Fish Lake

Mt. McLoughlin
(9495 ft.)

Grizzly Peak
(5921 ft.)

Bear Cr.

Medford

Bear
Creek
Valley

Coleman Cr.

Wagner Cr.

Ashland

Wagner
Butte

Mt. Ashland
(7533 ft.)

Emigrant Cr.

2/9

2/10

2/11

2/8

Pilot Rock
(5910 ft.)

2/8

2/9

Little
Applegate R.

Yale Cr.

2/11

2/15

SISKIYOU
MOUNTAINS

OREGON
CALIFORNIA

Applegate R.

Applegate R.

SECTION THREE

Siskiyou Summit to
the Upper Rogue River

0   Scale   5
miles

February "10" [9]: this is certainly a fine Country and probably no Climate in any Country equal to it.

Descending from Siskiyou Summit (center-background) into the upper Bear Creek Valley during unseasonably mellow weather, the chief trader was quite impressed with the area around present Ashland, Oregon (right). This southeastward view shows the foothills of the Siskiyou Mountains (right) and the Cascade Range (left). On February "10," Ogden would have advanced along the near side of Bear Creek (from the center to the right edge of the photograph). (Photo by author)

---

tral Point, Ogden was so favorably impressed by the area's rich soil and mild climate that his journal almost reads like an early Jackson County Chamber of Commerce promotional brochure. It is clear that the brigade had happened into the "Rogue Valley" during one of its typical February "false springs,"[37] a usually short-lived period of relatively warm, gentle weather during which the open oak woodlands can sprout a thick carpet of wildflowers and green grass.

FEBRUARY "10" [9][1827]: . . . *this morning fine warm weather. We started at 8 A.M. and proceeded on untill 2 P.M. when we encamped on a large Fork form'd by a number of small Streams which we crossed in our travels this day ≤ and in many of them not long since there were Beaver . . . this is certainly a fine Country and probably no Climate in any Country equal to it, the Indians inform us the winter is now over and I am almost inclined to believe them from the singing of Birds of all kinds, grass green and at its full growth Flowers in blossom certainly entitles them to be credited but we are yet in February ≤ with the exception of Mountains which appear at some distance from us the Highest Hills are without Snow ≤ if we may judge from the heat at present how it is in Summer certainly then it must be great ≦ from the dry state of the roads it does not appear as they are annoyed with rain but probably all seasons are not alike ≦ be it so but at present it is certainly fine weather and certainly a country well adapted from its Soil and timber (Oaks and Pine) for cultivation. The natives inform us that Deer are abundant in the hills and Mountains . . . from their being all well clad in Leather I can well believe them . . . Arrow quivers made of Beaver Skins also their Caps . . . they were most anxious in directing where to find them observing there were but few in the small Streams but in the large River [the Rogue] they were numerous . . . so far as I could see in advance there was not the appearance of any. . . . Here we are now amongst the tribe of Sastise or (Castise) it was this Tribe that was represented to our party of last year and also to us as being most hostilily inclined towards us* [38] *≦ so far we cannot say what their intentions may be ≦ we have not seen more than 30 and their conduct has been friendly. . . . Course this day West ≦ Distance 15 miles.*

Ogden, probably with most of his trappers in advance, began this day by travelling down Hill Creek towards its confluence with Emigrant Creek. He possibly crossed the very low divide between Hill Creek and Neil

---

February "10" [9]: With the exception of Mountains which appear at some distance from us the Highest Hills are without Snow.

This southward view of the city of Ashland and snow-dusted Mt. Ashland (center skyline) shows Ogden's route along the near side of Bear Creek (left-to-right across the center of the photograph). The brigade probably travelled along the edge of the bluffs that overlook the Bear Creek floodplain. (Photo by author)

Creek to the northwest, near the place where Oregon Highway 66 crosses today. His course would have been generally northwest as he crossed the various upper tributaries, the "number of small Streams" of Bear Creek. Bear Creek is formed by the confluence of Emigrant Creek and Neil Creek, about two miles east of downtown Ashland. For about three miles below this point it flows west-northwest (thereby essentially agreeing with Ogden's direction of "West") before taking a northwest course to the Rogue River. His "15 miles" of travel would have brought him a mile or two below the mouth of Ashland Creek, where he camped.[39] Based on a later journal entry, Ogden's path probably now lay on the east side of Bear Creek, along the low bluffs that overlook the stream.

If, as the 1961 edition states, Ogden had been descending the Little Applegate, he would now have been just below the mouth of Glade Creek, at an elevation of around 3,000 feet. Here the Little Applegate River still occupies a steep, narrow canyon, one that is heavily forested with conifers. The Bear Creek campsite, in contrast, was below the 1,800-foot level, by this point within the relatively wide valley bottom. His bucolic descriptions certainly tally with the latter location in the Bear Creek Valley. The snow-covered "Mountains which appear at some distance" most likely were Mount Ashland and Wagner Butte, the major Siskiyou peaks that dominate the southern Bear Creek Valley. The "Highest Hills . . . without Snow" would be the southwest-aspect slopes of Grizzly Peak and Mt. Baldy, the foothills of the Cascade Range that enclose the valley along the northeast. Their grassy slopes are usually snow-free throughout most of the winter. The "Flowers in blossom" would indicate that grouseflower (*Synthyris laniformus*), purple-eyed grass (*Sisyrinchium douglasii*), toothwort (*Cardamine integrifolia*), buttercup (*Ranunculus spp.*) and other typically early-blooming species of the low elevation oak woodlands were by then in flower.[40]

As Ogden noted, the brigade was still among the Shasta Indians. This particular band, the "Ikirukatsu," inhabited the southern-most portion of the Bear Creek Valley.[41] To the north were the Upland Takelma, or "Latgawa." Contrary to the warning given to Ogden by jealous Klamath Indians, the Shasta were peacably inclined towards the Hudson's Bay Company trappers. The Shasta, in turn, would do their best to cast their Takelma neighbors in an unfavorable light.

FEBRUARY "11" [10]: *We started at an early hour ≦ we had not proceeded more than four miles when we joined part of our Trappers who informed us that we were in the centre of their Traps, we then encamped. . . . they have been here two nights and the first from 60 Traps only three [beaver] were taken and last night 20 odd so this is a convincing proof they are very wild. . . . Distance 4 miles ≦ Course WNW . . . Racoons are certainly numerous in this Country ≦ scarcely a day passes but some are taken in the traps.*

February "11" [10]: We started at an early hour ≦ we had not proceeded more than four miles when we joined part of our Trappers . . . we then encamped.

After leaving the Ashland vicinity, Ogden camped for several days near present Talent (center of photograph). This southeastward view (taken from Barneburg Hill in Medford) shows Wagner Butte on the extreme right. Siskiyou Summit is located beyond the center skyline. (Photo by author)

Ogden's group followed Bear Creek to the vicinity of present-day Talent, probably camping near the mouth of Wagner Creek. The chief trader was discouraged to learn that the natives hunted beaver quite heavily, making his quarry that much more timid and difficult to trap. The expedition camped near Talent for four days. (The 1961 edition places this camp at the confluence of Yale Creek and the Little Applegate River.) While most of the men went off to reconnoiter the local streams, some of them apparently remained in camp to repair broken traps.

FEBRUARY "12" [11]: *The croaking of Frogs last night certainly surprised me ≦ this is certainly an early season for them to be in motion . . . we shall soon have rain. . . . I gave orders to the Trappers to visit [their traps] but not to raise untill tomorrow when I shall raise Camp. . . . —[the Shasta Indians] say the Stream we are now encamped on has no connection with the Clammitte River that it [the Klamath drainage] takes a*

Southern whereas this [the Rogue drainage] takes a Western Course ⪬ so far as regard the latter this is correct as you advance from the Forks [Emigrant Creek and Neil Creek?] that discharge into it becomes a large River [Ogden had not yet seen the Rogue] and as far as we have been still continues to increase we know nothing of the Clammitte River we must seek for it—if the above information should prove correct as regards the River I shall and I may add all will be pleased . . . all the Indians agree in saying the farther you advance the more Beaver you will find . . . we are still in the vicinty of the Mountains [Wagner Butte, visible a few miles to the south] . . . I must say our expectations now are sanguine more than when we first made our appearance in this Country.

February "12" [11]: the Stream we are now encamped on . . . continues to increase . . . I must say our expectations now are sanguine more than when we first made our appearance in this Country.

Encouraged by the "beaver sign" along Bear Creek (seen here in a downstream view at Medford's Barnett Street bridge), Ogden looked forward to exploring the Indians' "beaver-rich" Rogue River to the north. (Photo by author)

FEBRUARY "*13*" [*12*]: *We passed rather an unpleasant night* ≲ *about mid night Mr. McKay roused me from my sleep and informed me that an Indian [probably Shasta] has just arrived and informed him the Indians [probably Upland Takelma] in numbers had assembled together and were on the eve of attacking our Camp. . . . It is not my opinion they have any evil intentions towards us* ≲ *nor is it our intent at present from our want of knowledge of the Country* ≲ *our men scattered along the banks of the River* ≲ *ten men absent . . . [Indians] warning us* to be on our guard when we reach the next Tribe *with whom it appears they are at variance and consequently like all other Tribes I am acquainted with represent them as hostitily inclined towards us* ≲ *from all this I am inclined to believe it was a false report. . . . I sent orders to the rear party of the rear Trappers not to raise Camp untill I joined them tomorrow that we may not be too far scattered and to be on their guards* ≲ *and this warning I constantly repeat to them every time we meet. . . . Our [Shasta] Guides informed us that they did not intend to proceed any further with us* ≲ *on receiving this information we reminded them of their promise of substituting others in their place* ≲ *to this they promise fair and I believe will prevail on one to accompany us . . . having a Stream before us but not knowing what impediments we may meet with, it is prudent one should accompany us. In the evening the rear party of our Trappers arrived with 29 Beaver . . . altho a Mountainous country and we are not yet far from the sources of the River [Bear Creek] it [the fact that the local beaver pelts had such thin fur] is to me almost unaccountable excepting it be attributed to the mildness of the Climate.*

FEBRUARY "*14*" [*13*]: *I did not raise Camp. . . . One of the Trappers yesterday saw a domesticated Cat in a rather wild state* ≲ *he endeavored to secure it but in vain* ≲ *I presume it must have come from the Coast* ≲ *in that quarter all along they are in almost every village a dozen of them* ≲ *but how this one found its way in this distant quarter for all the Indians still persist in asserting they know nothing of the Sea . . . he must certanly lead a solitary life . . . but field mice are numerous all over the Plains.*

While Ogden pondered the question of his distance from the ocean, he also worried over the fate of Payette's party, then trapping somewhere well down the Klamath River from Cottonwood Creek. From the unease of his "Sastise" guides, Ogden was probably near or beyond the approximate dividing line between the Shasta and the Upland Takelma territory. The "rear party of Trappers" would have been exploring the upper reaches of the Emigrant Creek and Walker Creek drainages, perhaps ascending the foothills of the Cascades to reach the edge of the 4,500-foot high "Dead Indian Plateau," a broad volcanic upland of relatively gentle terrain. One of the trappers in the Bear Creek Valley reported seeing a "domesticated Cat";[42] if an accurate account, it was probable evidence of some form of contact with coastal villages. Ogden's reference to the numerous field mice "all over the Plains" again indicates the open, lightly wooded country of the Bear Creek Valley. Despite the possible threat from the "next Tribe"

February "15" [14]: at 9 A.M. we started still following down
the Fork [Bear Creek] . . . We travelled over a fine level
Country.

This northward view from the roof of Medford's Federal
Building shows the brigade's route (right-to-left) over the
"fine level Country" of the lower Bear Creek Valley. The
foothills of the Cascade Range are visible on the horizon.
Ogden would have passed through what is now Medford,
down the east side of Bear Creek. (Photo by author)

(the Upland Takelma), the brigade pushed on in search of beaver. The
next day's travels brought Ogden to the Rogue River. His journal entry for
that date is another particularly significant one for a correct interpretation
of his journey.

FEBRUARY "15" [14]: Fine clear weather, this morning the Horse Keeper in collecting
his Horses found one kill'd and three wounded by arrows. . . . from our want of
knowledge of the Country we are in and the Trappers scattered in different directions
prevents me at present from making an example of some of them ≤ the only alternative left at present for us is to commence again our night guard . . . they certainly
evince a most malicious disposition towards us and if not checked and that soon our
Scalps will soon share the fate of our Horses. . . . we loaded our Horses and at 9 AM
we started still following down the Fork when within a mile of its discharge in a large
River equal in size to the Willimatte we cross'd over [to the west side of Bear Creek]

*February "15" [14]: a large River equal in size to the
Willimatte . . . a fine looking Stream well wooded with Poplar
Aspine and Willows. . . . this River I have nam'd Sastise
River.*

After reaching the Rogue River, shown here from its
south bank a few miles downstream from the mouth of
Bear Creek, Ogden camped near this spot for a week
while his trappers reconnoitered the "Sastise" and its
nearby tributaries. (Photo by author)

---

*and soon after reached it [the Rogue] and when we descended for four miles when the
Trappers informed me I was in the advance of their Traps we of course encamped, we
made a long days march having travelled from nine in the morning until five in the
evening ≲ but the distance was not in proportion to the time from the state of the roads
≲ worse they cannot be the last three days of rain have done them no good . . . This is
certainly a fine looking Stream well wooded with Poplar Aspine and Willows and from
its depth it must either be well supplyed with tributary Streams or its rise must be far
distant ≲ we shall in course of time ascertain it—this River I have nam'd Sastise
River also a mount equal in height to Mount Hood or Vancouver [Mt. Jefferson] I
have nam'd Mount Sistise ["Sastise"] its bearings by our Compass from our present*

encampment East South East ≦ I have given these names from the Tribe of Indians who are well known by all the neighbouring Tribes . . . by giving English names it often tends to lead strangers astray. . . . We travelled over a fine level Country and on reaching this River we saw two small Herds of White tail Deer . . . Distance this day 15 miles ≦ Course West North West . . . One of the Trappers reported . . . he met with three Indians who on seeing him strung their Bows and mad[e] preparations for sending him a few Arrows. . . . At this season dead Salmon are most numerous in all the Small Rivers and the Natives are busily employed in collecting them no doubt

---

February "15" [14]: a mount equal in height to Mount Hood . . . I have nam'd Mount Sistise ["Sastise"].

Ogden's initial sighting of "Mount Sastise" (Mt. McLoughlin) would have been at or very near this view-point from lower Bear Creek, near the present city of Central Point. (Photo by author)

for food. . . . the Indians even go so far as to select them in a putrid state giving them the preference ≤ what a depraved taste. . . . For us to attempt finding [the Payette party] is impossable as we know not what part of the Mountains they cross'd but they have not that excuse as our Camp track [the main party's trail] will be visible for a long time ≤ nor were we aware these waters did not discharge in the Clammitte River . . . but in due time we shall ascertain the point.

After crossing to the west side of Bear Creek, probably about a mile downstream from Central Point, Ogden reached the Rogue River (the "large River equal in size to the Willimatte") in the afternoon, and descended along its south bank to his camp not far downstream from the present Gold Ray Dam. His overall course direction for this day would have been northwest, although the final few miles indeed would have been to the west-northwest. The brigade's route this morning evidently had passed along the east side of Bear Creek, through or near the present sites of Phoenix, Medford, and Central Point—that is, over the "fine level Country" of the lower Bear Creek Valley. The trappers had entered the heart of Upland Takelma territory. Ogden related that one man was threatened by three Indians of the new tribe but that no violence resulted. He also remarked on the plentiful "dead Salmon" in the local streams, and commented with disgust on the natives' preference for taking those fish "in a putrid state."

The 1961 edition identifies the "large River" as the main stem of the Applegate, but the actual course of Ogden's "Sastise River," as described in the following three weeks of his journal entries, would definitely disagree. Ogden was clearly describing the Rogue, the "fine looking Stream well wooded with Poplar Aspine and Willows."[43] Later journal entries certainly indicate a river with the width and depth of the Rogue, not the significantly smaller Applegate.

The "mount equal in height to Mount Hood," could only be Mount McLoughlin. Although it is under 10,000 feet in elevation (Mt. Hood, in contrast, rises well over 11,000 feet above sea level), the symmetrical cone of Mt. McLoughlin is by far the dominant feature of this section of the Cascade Range, and it would have impressed the chief trader as being similar in height to Mt. Hood. It first became visible to Ogden on this day, as the brigade travelled alongside Bear Creek, just east of what is now the city of Central Point. (It likely could have been visible to him in late December from the Upper Klamath Lake area, but he made no mention of it; it was raining and snowing at the time, and the mountain was no doubt obscured from view.) Mt. McLoughlin is situated almost due east from the probable location of Ogden's Rogue River camp; his recorded bearing of "East South East" is not that significant an error.[44] Ogden named the snow-covered peak "Mount Sistise" (certainly a mis-copy of "Sastise"] after the Indians among whom he had been travelling for the past two weeks. It becomes apparent, then, that the *present* Mt. Shasta was *not* visible to Ogden on this day—and this remains true whether his route lay along Bear Creek *or* the Applegate River; Mt. Shasta is nowhere visible from the latter stream. As stated previously, he never gave a specific name to the 14,162-foot high Mt. Shasta of today. It evidently first received this name several years later.[45] Thus, today's Mount McLoughlin was the original "Mount Shasta" ("Sastise") of Peter Ogden.

FEBRUARY "16" [15]: *the Rivers are rising fast ≲ the Trappers are alarmed. . . . they have visited a Small Fork near by ≲ found a few Beaver ≲ complain of the unsteady state of the Water and Natives most numerous bold and Insolant . . . they appear determined to oblige us to leave their Country.*

FEBRUARY "17" [16]: *. . . Some Traps were visited but those beyond the forks [the confluence of Bear Creek and the Rogue?] the Trappers could not reach them the Water having risen nearly three feet perpendicular and in the main Stream, it fell in the same proportion ≲ but should we have two days of fine weather it will rise rapidly and the Small forks will fall in proportion. . . . we sent off one of our [Shasta] Guides to discover the Indians and by fair means to induce some of them to our Camp so as to obtain some information from them relative to the Country for beyond this in any direction our Guides are entirely ignorant.*

FEBRUARY "18" [17]: *. . . Three Men commenced making a Canoe and I am in hopes they will complete it tomorrow so as to enable them to crooss [cross] over to sett the Traps, there is a fine large Fork on the oposite side a short distance from this and we are in hopes of finding Beaver in it. Our messenger returned from his errand and informs us the Indians will assemble and pay us their respects tomorrow . . . from their late conduct they appear to wish to remain at variance with us. . . . Day after day passes and still no accounts . . . of our absent men.*

FEBRUARY "19" [18]: *Our expected Indians did not make their appearance—the men finished their Canoe and cross'd over the River also four more on Rafts . . . waters are now gradually subsiding . . . numerous Flocks of Wild Fowl consisting of Grey and White Geese Bustards & Swans pass'd by bending their course to the Westward.*

FEBRUARY "20" [19]: *. . . [beaver] fur can almost be compared to Summer Beaver. . . . Ten Indians paid us a visit ≲ they denied having any knowledge or being any ways concerned in the killing of our Horses and express a wish to remain at peace with us.*

FEBRUARY "21" [20]: *Late last evening I was pleased to see seven of the nine absent men make their appearance but their success has not been so great . . . only 73 Beavers 9 Otters.*

FEBRUARY "22" [21]: *Last evening upwards of fifty Indians assembled near the Camp and sent two men in advance to inform us they wished to make peace with us ≲ they received our consent and soon after made their appearance ≲ this affair was soon*

Lower Table Rock, one of the landmarks Ogden never
mentioned. Ogden's omission likely was due simply to the
fact that, after roaming the volcanic tablelands of central
Oregon and northeastern California (where such sights
are common), this particular kind of feature did not seem
especially noteworthy. If Ogden's journal had referred to
the two basaltic mesas, Table Rocks, twentieth-century
historians would have had far less difficulty in retracing
the chief trader's route of travel. (Photo by author)

*settled at the expense of two Dozen Buttons. . . . After this ceremony was concluded
they amused the Camp with a dance ≤ in this they acquitted themselves as well as
Indians ever did. . . . We have this day 15 Beaver which completes our first thousand
and leaves us eight to commence our second with. . . . The Indians in this quarter
give us no hopes of finding any but inform us as we descend this River your progress*

will soon be arrested by I suppose the same chain of mountains our party had to contend with ⪅ it may be so but at present we must examine the upper part of this Stream before we think of decending.

Ogden stayed at his first Rogue River camp (probably near the eastern base of Gold Hill) for a full week, through February "22." During this period the heavy rains caused the river to rise considerably, and this wreaked havoc with trapping. Many of Ogden's trappers probably explored Antelope Creek, Little Butte Creek, and other "small Forks" to the east. Some of his men built a "canoe" (a dugout?) and rafts in order to cross to the north side of the Rogue to explore the "fine large Fork on the oposite side," which lay a short distance from the camp. This almost certainly would have been Sams Creek which drains "Sam's Valley" on the north side of the Table Rocks. Upper and Lower Table Rocks are two very prominent local landmarks, and it is curious that the chief trader made no mention of them in his Journal. These mesa-like formations, the remnants of a once-extensive Miocene basalt flow, would have been plainly visible to Ogden, rising just across the river from his camp. Perhaps after his previous travels among the rimrock- and mesa-studded sagebrush desert of the northern Great Basin and Snake River Plains, such geological phenomena were not particularly noteworthy to Ogden. Whatever the reason for the chief trader's silence, it is virtually certain that he saw the Table Rocks.[46]

During this week-long respite from travel, Ogden witnessed vast flocks of waterfowl flying overhead. These birds were probably following the Bear Creek Valley north, turning westward along the Rogue River before again shifting their course north to the Umpqua and Willamette valleys. Ogden brooded about the behavior of the "Natives most . . . Insolant," and he expressed anxiety over the fate of Payette. Late in the evening of February "20," Payette's party finally arrived in camp, apparently having backtracked up the Klamath River to Cottonwood Creek and then followed Ogden's trail to the Rogue. Undoubtedly relieved at their safe arrival, Ogden recorded their account of the lower Klamath River Country:

> *Villages built in the manner as the Indians of the Coast with Ceodar Plank sufficiently large to contain from 20 to 30 Families and on every point where it was possable to reach the River did they see Villages . . . and various trading articles such as Knives Axes and Tea Kettles the latter most numerous no doubt obtained from some American Ship . . . in four days they could reach the Sea. . . .*

Payette and his small group evidently had descended the Klamath River canyon into Karok territory, probably at least to the vicinity of Happy Camp. The trappers then "marched four days in the Mountains" (probably somewhere in the Siskiyous between Red Buttes on the northeast and Preston Peak to the southwest) before returning across the "cut Rocks" to the Klamath River.

The next evening, the Upland Takelma residents of the Table Rock area decided to make peace with these first white intruders. Ogden permitted a group of fifty Indians into camp; after receiving some trinkets ("two Dozen Buttons") the natives made peace and "amused the Camp with a dance."[47] Dissatisfied with the brigade's total take of 1,000 beaver pelts, Ogden decided that he "must examine the upper part of this Stream [the "Sastise" or Rogue River] before we think of descending." This leg of the journey took the brigade north into the headwaters of the Rogue.

FEBRUARY "23" [22]: . . . *weather has dismal appearance ≲ still we raised Camp and commenced ascending the Stream and proceeded on untill the afternoon when we encamped having joined part of the Trappers and also some on the oposite side of the River. On starting this morning we crossed over a fine large Fork which has been examined to its sources and has produced a few Beaver . . . Our road followed the banks of the River ≲ it certainly looks well being well lin'd with Willows and wood of different kind, Stream deep and rapids not numerous, the Country around us Mountainous and I am not of opinion we shall proceed far before our progress be arrested by rocks and Mountains. Our Course this day North Distance 15 miles ≲ roads bad . . . the two remaining men of the [Payette] party of nine made their appearance. . . . The soil along the Banks of the River is far from being good consisting of Sand and Gravel ≲ the very reverse to what we have seen for some time past.*

Above the Table Rocks, Ogden's course up the Rogue would have been almost due north. Approximately fifteen miles of travel would have placed the brigade's camp in the vicinity of Shady Cove, perhaps almost as far upstream as Trail Creek. The main group ascended along the left (south and east) bank of the river, crossing the mouth of Little Butte Creek (the "fine large Fork") soon after starting. Trappers previously had examined that stream "to its sources," possibly as far as Fish Lake. Ogden's comment about the sandy, gravelly banks of the river is still an appropriate description of this section of the flood-prone Rogue, especially near and above Shady Cove.

The 1961 version would have Ogden ascending the Applegate River, but this would entail a travel route due *south*. Could this again be actually a case of mis-copy—"north" for south? Possibly, but doubtful; Ogden's later entries, including those for the brief period when he was actually in the Applegate River drainage, make it clear that he reconnoitered the upper Rogue during late February.

Ogden camped somewhere near Shady Cove for three days, during intermittent heavy snowfall, while small parties of men trapped the tributaries of the upper Rogue. Four of Ogden's trappers left with intentions of "making the Sources of the River," but they returned two days later, their progress halted by the "depth of Snow." These men reported that the "upper part of the River where they could reach it was covered with ice and no want of Rocks." The foregoing description strongly hints that the scouts had skirted Cascade Gorge on the south side, and may have reached the vicinity of Prospect, perhaps as far as Union Creek. Discouraged by this news (and by the scarcity of beaver), Ogden determined to "return

This northward view of the upper Rogue River's gorge, just below the town of Prospect, shows the rugged canyon country that would have halted the progress of Ogden's four scouts. They passed along the opposite edge of the canyon. Due to the "depth of Snow" somewhere in the vicinity of Prospect or Union Creek, they turned back, failing to make "the Sources of the River." (Photo by author)

back our steps and bid adieu to this cold and Mountainous Country." The brigade headed back downstream, having penetrated to within a few leagues of Crater Lake, on February "27."

> FEBRUARY "27" [26]: . . . we started early and reached the Fork [Little Butte Creek] we crossed on the 23rd [22nd] and encamped ≦ roads as usual very bad.

Backtracking along the Rogue, Ogden spent this night just below the mouth of Little Butte Creek, probably near present-day Tou Velle State Park.

> FEBRUARY "28" [27]: Weather mild ≦ no Snow in this quarter ≦ the Snow we had has been Rain here. We rais'd Camp and followed down the Stream [the Rogue] untill the discharge of the Fork we crossed on the 15th [14th: Bear Creek, which the brigade crossed just prior to first reaching the Rogue] . . . encamped ≦ here we found the seven men who started three days since in advance with three Beavers. On reaching the encampment all the Trappers started down the Stream. . . . one of them kill'd a Grey Squirrel of a large size and remarkable long and bushy tail.

The brigade probably camped at or near its initial Rogue River bivouac, below Gold Ray Dam and near the north base of Blackwell Hill. Staying here one more day, Ogden dispatched a group under McKay and Payette back up the Bear Creek Valley and over the Siskiyous. They were to trap some of the Klamath River tributaries seen by Payette. The chief trader, determined to continue downstream, sent several men to scout the Rogue's lower course. They returned the same day, reporting "favourably of the River [they] said Country so far as they had been as far as they could see there appears no Mountains to prevent us from advancing." Ogden's scouts evidently descended the Rogue to the vicinity of Grants Pass.

SECTION FOUR:
Down the Rogue and North to the Coquille

DURING THIS LEG of the trip Ogden continued down the south bank of the Rogue River from the Bear Creek Valley to the Grants Pass area. There he crossed to the north side of the river and travelled "cross-country" to the drainage of Cow Creek, a tributary of the Umpqua River, which he descended for some distance. The brigade then apparently made a brief visit to the Middle Fork of the Coquille before returning to the Umpqua River drainage.

In most respects, this is by far the most confusing section of the chief trader's route. Ogden's writing style begins to show signs of his fatigue and discouragement. On those occasions when the journal is not overly laconic, it contains an exasperating number of references to unspecified "Mountains," "Forks," "Streams," and "Rivers." Ogden often used the latter three terms indiscriminately for the same feature, and it becomes necessary at times to make an "educated guess" as to just what body of water he meant. In short, it is a challenge to interpret this section of Ogden's itinerary. The 1961 edition offers the reader few geographical guideposts, and those that are given often conflict with Ogden's information. One must remember that the brigade was, indeed, in an area that today still can seem a bewildering country—a maze of twisting river canyons, the ultimate courses of which Ogden could only surmise. Was his "Sastise River" (the Rogue) a tributary of the "Clammitte," or was it an independent stream? One day he seemed certain of the answer; a few days later the report of his scouts apparently threw him back into a geographic quandry. Nevertheless, if the reader accepts the validity of the previously

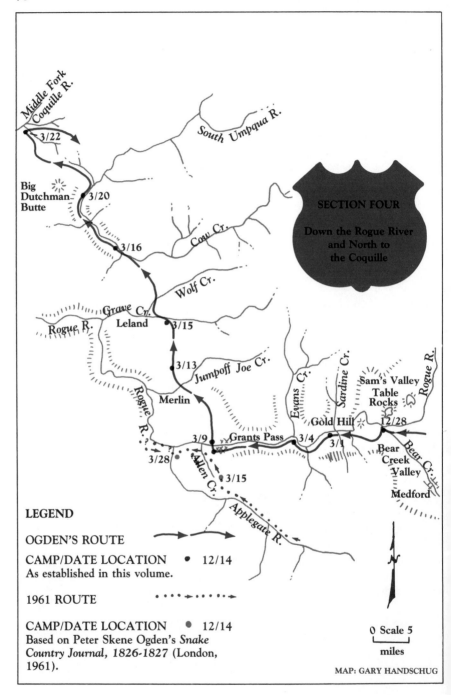

Middle Fork Coquille R.

South Umpqua R.

3/22

Big Dutchman Butte • 3/20

SECTION FOUR

Down the Rogue River and North to the Coquille

• 3/16

Cow Cr.

Wolf Cr.

Grave Cr.

Rogue R.

Leland • 3/15

• 3/13

Jumpoff Joe Cr.

Evans Cr.

Sardine Cr.

Sam's Valley
Table Rocks

Rogue R.

Rogue R.

Merlin

Gold Hill · 12/28

3/9 • Grants Pass 3/4 • 3/1

3/28 •

Bear Creek Valley

Bear Cr.

Allen Cr.

• 3/15

Medford

Applegate R.

LEGEND

OGDEN'S ROUTE

CAMP/DATE LOCATION • 12/14
As established in this volume.

1961 ROUTE

CAMP/DATE LOCATION • 12/14
Based on Peter Skene Ogden's *Snake Country Journal, 1826-1827* (London, 1961).

0 Scale 5

miles

MAP: GARY HANDSCHUG

described Bear Creek Valley-upper Rogue River route, the general path of later travel becomes much easier to follow. Ogden's journal entries for this section provide just sufficient spoor for us to retrace most of his trail.

> MARCH 1 [1827]: We had a rainy night but a fine day. At an early hour we were in motion and at nine Mr. McKay with 13 men seperated from us. . . . At 11 A.M. we started ≶ my party now numbers 24 ≶ on starting we left the River taking an East [mis-copy for "West"] Course two miles when we crossed over a long point and 1 P.M. we again reached the main Stream amongst Falls and Cascades ≶ on the oposite side we saw a large Village containing six large Houses sufficiently so to contain upwards of 100 Indians but on seeing us preparing to encamp oposite their Village they soon left and ascended the hills with their Children and property. . . . We had but a few Traps sett the greater part from the sudden rising of the water last night nearly 2 1/2 feet perpendicular could not be found. . . . Distance this day six miles ≶ worse roads cannot be found—the River here appears to take a South West Course

Taking his leave from McKay and Payette, Ogden travelled about six miles down the Rogue. The journal's reference to an "East Course" is definitely a copy error for "West"; neither the Rogue River nor any other major stream in this portion of the Pacific Northwest, including the Applegate, flows eastward. In addition, later in this same entry (as well as in succeeding entries) Ogden mentions the river's "South West" course. Ogden's actual route away from and then back to the Rogue's south bank this day would have been almost due west. The brigade left the river near its camp and crossed over a "long point" for two miles. The trappers most likely passed over the low saddle between Gold Hill and Blackwell Hill, or possibly over the south slope of Blackwell Hill (the present route of Interstate 5). They returned to the Rogue above the mouth of Kane Creek and reached the narrow, whitewater gorge just east of the present town of Gold Hill. A short distance below this stretch of the river, the Rogue indeed takes a "South West" course as far as one can see.

Here, near the present site of the town of Gold Hill, Ogden saw a large village "containing six large Houses" on the opposite (north or west) bank. This would have been the Takelma settlement of "Dilomi," reported by later sources to have been "an unusually large village."[48] Upon seeing the strangers, the inhabitants fled into the hills to the north. Ogden's men, discouraged by the continued rapid fluctuations in the river level ("2 1/2 feet perpendicular" overnight), decided to cross the Rogue and investigate the suddenly deserted community.

> MARCH 2: This day commenced with rain and continued all day ≶ we did not attempt starting. . . . Some of the men who succeeded in crossing the River yesterday went to the Village ≶ they found only two men remaining with one Woman, in their Village they saw a Sickle and two China Bowls ≶ from whom they procured theses articles we

could not learn . . . have travelled from the Coast and probably procured from some Ships passing by ≤ they would not part with either, the Sickle they make use of as a substitute for a Knife and the Bowls are preserved as ornaments ≤ they would not part with either appearing to lay considerable value on both, this is certainly a convincing proof they or Tribes not far distant have had intercourse with Ships or Tradors but in my opinion with the former or probably with the Spaniards in some of their trading excursions have ascended a part of this Stream ≤ but as we advance we may see more and obtain more correct information . . . some distance below there is a large Fork which from appearances we are in hope of finding Beaver ≤ the Country on the oposite side is also less woody and hilly and Grass more abundant. During the night the water fell 14 inches and this day it has risen ten perpendicular.

Camped on the south side of the Rogue, Ogden mentioned the marked difference in vegetation between the drier, grassy, south-aspect slopes across the river from him and the forested, north-aspect hillsides that rose behind his camp.[49] Variability in the Rogue's water level continued to plague the trappers. Some of them crossed the river to the Takelma village, where they found several interesting trade items. The "China Bowls" were probably either "Spode" transfer-print earthenwares from England or low value "Canton" porcelain wares from China, brought to Oregon in European or American trading ships.[50] Ogden's speculation on the source of these trade goods ("Spaniards") soon proved to be erroneous; he later learned that such items most likely originated from none other than his employer, the Hudson's Bay Company.   •

Based on Ogden's entry of two days later, the "large Fork . . . some distance below" is probably Evans Creek. The main camp remained at the Gold Hill rapids through the next day.

MARCH 3: . . . *Fair or foul tomorrow we must start otherwise we must start killing our Horses for food. One of my men by orders swam across the River and after a long search succeeded in finding a Canoe which he cross'd over leaving the full value of it in the same place . . . the owners will find and give them a favourable opinion of our good intentions. . . . In the afternoon six men started in advance with Traps and two with their Rifles in quest of Deer.*

MARCH 4: . . . *at ten we started and followed down the Stream and continued descending untill 2 P.M. when we reach'd a large Fork on the oposite side of the River and encamped. So far from appearances the River is almost one continued Rapid and not altogether well adapted for Beaver ≤ there is however a sufficiency of timber but in my opinion the descend is too great ≤ but in the present state of the Water it may appear greater than it is. . . . Distance 10 miles ≤ Course S West.*

Ogden seems to have estimated his mileage this day, the fourth, quite correctly. Following the Rogue southwest for over six miles to its major bend at the mouth of Foots Creek, the brigade then would have turned northwest for another four miles, arriving even with the mouth of Evans Creek (the "large Fork on the oposite side"). The actual compass direction from Gold Hill to Evans Creek is almost due west. Ogden's camp was situated just across the "Sastise" from the present city of Rogue River. He remained here for the next two days while some of his men crossed the Rogue and explored upper Evans Creek. Other trappers reconnoitered downriver. One of Ogden's men, evidently having ascended the Evans Creek drainage, reported seeing the "tracks of two Horses of last Fall." Ogden was "at a loss to know":

who this can be who travels with Horses in this Quarter for since our leaving the Clammitte not one or the track of one have we seen and the natives . . . from their gazing at ours made us comprehend they were the first [horses] they had seen.

March 4: . . . at ten we started and followed down the [Stream] . . . when we reach'd a large Fork on the oposite side of the River and encamped.

This upstream view of the Rogue at the town of Rogue River looks back on Ogden's course along the south bank (right side in photograph). The brigade camped very near here while some of the men crossed over to the north bank and explored Evans Creek, the "large Fork on the oposite side." (Photo by author)

These tracks were probably made by members of the small party under Jean Baptiste Depaty and Michel Laframboise, who were attached to Alexander Roderick McLeod's 1826–27 "Umpqua" Brigade. Travelling south from Fort Vancouver, McLeod trapped much of the Coquille River drainage and even journeyed south along the Oregon coast as far as the mouth of the Rogue River. The "interior" detachment under Depaty and Laframboise trapped in the Umpqua River drainage and briefly crossed into the Rogue River basin, evidently travelling at least as far south as Jumpoff Joe Creek.[51] The headwaters of Evans Creek and Jumpoff Joe Creek share a rather low-elevation watershed divide. Consequently, some of McLeod's trappers could well have ridden across this ridge into the upper Evans Creek Valley in January of 1827, where their tracks were seen only two months later by Ogden's men.

> MARCH 7: . . . At an early hour we started and continued following down the Stream untill late in the afternoon when we overtook nearly all the Trappers ≶ they report they have reached the discharge of this River into the Clammitte River not more than a mile from our present Encampment ≶ altho the Indians in the upper part reported it had no communication with it I was of a contrary opinion ≶ indeed it was almost impossable two such large River[s] should flow nearly in the same Course and not connect together sooner or later it now forms a large River . . . numerous Islands [sand and gravel bars?] and more appearance of Beaver than they have seen in any other part of this Country. . . . [trappers] have been but a short distance down the Stream and saw no rapids and the Country level ≶ this River or Sasty Fork is almost from its sources or from where we returned [near the mouth of Bear Creek] more or less one continued rapid ≶ well wooded ≶ may average an eigth of a mile in width ≶ deep banks ≶ low and in many parts stony soil at least from our separation encampment [near the mouth of Bear Creek, where Ogden parted from McKay] to here gravelly Country particularly our two last encampments ≶ woody, Oaks and Pines of different kinds and a few Cedar Trees well stock'd with Black Tail Deer and no doubt in the Mountains Red Deer . . . in a word it is a bold Stream containing a few scattered Beaver a fine Country rich in Timber and Animals good Pasture for Horses ≶ Climate rather too moist and natives so far as we can judge from appearances at least at this season not very numerous and the few there are very wild. . . . Mountains may also arrest our progress ≶ in fact we know not what there is in advance for us, in our rear we have little or nothing to expect.

Continuing down the Rogue, Ogden entered the site of the present city of Grants Pass, and probably encamped east of the mouth of Sand Creek, possibly near the western city limits. His advance trappers brought back reports of the river's "discharge . . . into the Clammitte River" not more than a mile downstream; the actual distance was probably at least twice that. They had actually seen the confluence of the Rogue and the *Applegate* Rivers; probably none of the party had seen the latter river before this date. Although Ogden did not visit the Applegate for several weeks after this date, he continued to think of it as being the Klamath, until he had seen and reconnoitered the stream for himself. After this time, Ogden must have speculated that he was on an entirely different river, for he no longer referred to it as the "Clammitte." The 1961 edition also puts Ogden near the confluence of the Applegate and the Rogue on March 7. How-

---

March 7: this River . . . [is] well wooded. . . . in a word it is a bold Stream. . . . a fine Country rich in Timber. . . . March 9: at an early hour we were in motion and with the assistance of two small Canoes at 4 P.M. all was safe across.

Ogden crossed the Rogue River (probably quite near this spot in the city of Grants Pass) on March 9. His course then lay to the north (left), toward "Umpqua Country." (Photo by author)

ever, his purported approach to this locality would, of course, have been downstream along the Applegate (having followed an almost continually northwest course after having crossed the Siskiyous at Siskiyou Gap).

Preparing to cross the "Sasty Fork" to the north side, Ogden here wrote at length about the river he had been following. The 1961 version would apply Ogden's description of the deep river, "an eighth of a mile in width," to the Applegate, but this clearly is not the case. The chief trader's "Sasty" (or "Sastise") was the Rogue River, which he crossed two days later.

> MARCH 8: *In the evening the three Trappers who have been a considerable distance down the River arrived with 13 Beaver and report as follows, From whence we turned [northwest?] no appearance of Beaver ≦ Rapids numerous ≦ River bare of wood ≦ also saw a Camp of Indians with the Chief one of them conversed in the Umpqua Language and obtained from him the following information [Ogden paraphrases:] the Umpqua River is far from this our neighbors trade with them occasionally and it is from them we obtain Knives and Axes which we barter for Beaver and Hyequas [dentalium shell], this accounts for our trading articles reaching this quarter and no doubt by the same means farther still, in regard to Beaver in the lower part of this River you will find none ≦ it is rocky and stony but at no great distance from this is another large River well stocked with Beaver, the Indians make Robes of them [some other Indians then arrived at Ogden's camp] . . . these Indians also informed us that there was a large River well stock'd in Beaver and only in one respect do not agree that is in regard to the distance we may be from it ≦ the former informed that we could reach it in three days and the latter say not in less than eight ≦ this is certainly a wide difference as regards time; but probably they have never seen it and their information may be derived from report . . . but before we can start it will be necessary to procure Guides and collect the trappers who are at present scattered . . . we shall be detained three or four days ere we will be in readiness . . . if the weather be fair tomorrow we shall endeavor to cross all over the Sasty River and not as I at first intended the Clammitte River ≦ this will be double trouble but if we find Beaver we will consider ourselves well repaid for our trouble.*

The Indians' report of a well-stocked beaver stream to the north turned Ogden's attentions away from exploring the lower "Sasty" (and thereby reaching its confluence with the "Clammitte," actually the Applegate River). Despite his misgivings about crossing the Rogue, even the hint of beaver was enough to cause Ogden to change course.[52] The trappers evidently had made contact with a River Takelma ("Dagelma") village somewhere below Grants Pass. The Indians possessed "Knives and Axes," apparently HBC trade goods that they probably had obtained through Umpqua intermediaries to the north.

> MARCH 9: . . . *at an early hour we were in motion and with the assistance of two small Canoes at 4 P.M. all was safe across ≦ I was rather uneasy about our Horses*

but all escaped [harm] and no sooner were a Cross and our Huts made when the Rain commenced and continued untill late in the evening . . . I sent men to find . . . to bring the Chief here . . . in the interim the remainder of the Trappers are not idle and we have a number of green skins . . . even our Leather Tents are now in rotten state . . . all the rain we have had lately has been Snow in the Mountains and I apprehend Mr. McKay will meet with detention.

Ogden and his party crossed the Rogue, probably between present downtown Grants Pass and Schroeder Park, without mishap. While they waited for their guide and several other men who were still absent, the trappers and their women occupied themselved by dressing the wet, "green" pelts.

MARCH 10: *. . . no account of the Men on the main Stream ≦ I am anxious about them and should they not arrive tomorrow I shall be under the necessity of leaving them ≦ now the Indians are becoming numerous and troublesome*

MARCH 11: *. . . the Indians have all scattered themselves and we cannot procure one to Guide us this places us rather in an awkward situation and I feel at a loss how to act . . . it is my opinion should there be a River it must discharge in the main Stream and we cannot but find it without the assistance of Indians ≦ still it would be an advantage to us to have one [a guide] . . . Freemen . . . the greater part would wish themselves out of this Country. . . . So far Beaver are but thinly scattered over this Country, one small Stream in the Snake Country would formerly have produced nearly as many.*

MARCH 12: *Altho I was fully determined last night [to leave] . . . rain prevented us even from making the attempt. . . . in the morning I sent three men down the main Stream in quest of a Guide and they succeeded in procuring one, this certainly should the fellow not escape be of a great advantage . . . he like all we have seen represent the River as Rich in Beaver and the Natives numerous ≦ probably they are at variance with them ≦ this may be the cause of their not wishing to Guide us there.*

MARCH 13: *. . . at 10 A.M. we started with our Guide during the night I strictly guarded him . . .—on starting we left the Sasty River or Fork in our rear taking West N West Course for 8 miles when we advanced 3 miles Course due West and encamped near by a lofty range of mountains . . . this day the Country on all sides appears the reverse of being a level one ≦ particularly towards the Main Stream which appears to take a South West [mis-copy for North West?] Course and am now of the opinion had we continued following it we would have had some trouble ≦ the Indians . . . represented it as impossible and this I am almost now inclined to believe to be correct ≦ this day we crossed over three small plains well stock'd with Camass Roots in one of them we saw several Men and Women employed in drying roots. . . . without him [the guide] we would certainly have had not only a bad but also a Mountainous road ≦ this with his assistance we have avoided—all along our track this day wood of different kinds and the White Pine of an extraordinary size.*

The brigade's path generally paralleled the present route of Interstate 5 north of Grants Pass. As stated previously, although Ogden's men had reported that the "Clammitte" (actually the Applegate) was but one mile below their river crossing, Ogden did not personally visit that stream during these several days; the distance was probably considerably greater than that.[53] After leaving the Rogue, the brigade probably camped somewhere in the vicinity of Merlin. Ogden's "lofty range of mountains" may have been Walker Mountain and Mount Sexton, to the northeast and north respectively, but he probably was referring to the much more rugged-appearing peaks of the Siskiyous visible to the west—peaks that, possibly unknown to Ogden at this point, were actually located across the Rogue River from his viewpoint. The three "small plains well stock'd with Camass Roots" were some of the small, grassy openings found in the oak-pine woodlands along Louse Creek and Jumpoff Joe Creek. Ogden mentioned the "White Pine of an extraordinary size." Undoubtedly the trees that caught the chief trader's eye were the locally common, large-diameter sugar pine (*Pinus lambertiana*) with their tremendous cones.

The next day, March "14," Ogden spent in camp. Six of his trappers left, evidently to scout Louse Creek and Jumpoff Joe Creek. Although they hardly qualify as "Rivers," that is how Ogden labeled the streams he had crossed after leaving the "Sasty." On the ides of March the brigade again progressed towards the hoped-for "beaver River." His journal entries for the next several days consistently give a more westerly course of travel than would seem to have been the actual case.[54]

> MARCH 15: . . . *we did not start untill the arrival of our Trappers in the rear who made their appearance at 10 A.M. . . . at 11 A.M. we started and soon after commenced ascending which continued for an hour when we again descended ≤ it was almost two [too] steep for our loaded Horses ≤ our Guide has no idea of a Horse track and supposes where he can pass it will answer for Horses ≤ after crossing the mountain we soon reached a large Fork . . . we encamped at 3 P.M. . . . Trappers reported rocks, stones, and Mountains in advance ≤ our Guide informed us towards its [the "Fork's"] discharge in the main stream [the Rogue] there were a few Beaver but the distance was great ≤ Our Course this day West North West ≤ Dist. 9 miles, Country woody and well stock'd in Red & Black tail deer ≤ Indians were seen by our Guide who brought them to the Camp ≤ these fellows informed us we would find Beaver in the big River . . . nor can I see what motives they have for deceiving us . . . however well do I know what an Indian calls a River of Beaver and probably we may be disappointed.*

The steep climb and descent this day would have been the Jumpoff Joe-Grave Creek divide, probably near where the Southern Pacific Railroad tunnel is located (west of Mt. Sexton Pass). Ogden must have reached Grave Creek above the site of Leland, and then descended that stream a short distance. Some of his trappers continued west along Grave Creek to look for beaver. They returned with discouraging news of "rocks, stones, and Mountains in advance." These men probably did not reach the creek's confluence with the Rogue (where Ogden's guide reported there were "a few Beaver"), but they did see the rugged summits of Brandy Peak, Sugarloaf Mountain, and other ridges off to the west.

The 1961 edition (p.94, n.1) places Ogden on Allen Creek, not Grave Creek. Allen Creek is a short, seasonal, *north*-draining stream that empties into the Rogue in the western part of Grants Pass. Having located Ogden at the juncture of the Rogue and the Applegate over a week previous, this March 15 site would not account for any of Ogden's intervening travels, including his crossing of the Rogue on March 9.

MARCH 16: . . . *two of the Freemen came forward and very politely requested leave to return to trap the Forks we left in our rear and then descend the Stream and rejoin us hereafter ≶ to this polite request I did not hesitate in refusing them. . . . On starting our Course due West which we followed to our encampment over certainly a most hilly and woody Country ≶ in fact it appears on all sides and as far as we can see one continued hill and mountain and altho many of them very high scarcely any snow ≶ we saw many Indian tracks ≶ one our Guide followed. . . . we had however in some parts recourse to our Axes ≶ we again this day cross'd over a Fork small but signs of Beaver—at one P.M. we reached a fine large one deep and well wooded and encamped ≶ on seeing it we all supposed this was the River our Guide had represented as being rich in Beaver but he says we are yet far from it . . . but the Trappers from what they have seen report favourably ≶ tomorrow it shall have fair trial and soon ascertain its value ≶ Dist 10 miles ≶ Course West. . . . well I venture to assert no Country can produce such a variety of Wood of all kinds nor finer timber suitable for all purposes.*

This day's course, "due West," actually would have turned to the northwest only a few hours after starting. Although the geography is confusing at this point, Ogden probably followed down Grave Creek to the mouth of Wolf Creek (the "Fork small"), which he then would have ascended a short distance before turning northwest to cross the high ridge that divides the Grave Creek drainage from that of Cow Creek to the north. Leaving Wolf Creek in the present vicinity of Pollard Station (a Southern Pacific Railroad siding), Ogden's brigade would have struggled over the summit of this ridge east of Hungry Hill and reached west-flowing Cow Creek, the "fine large [Fork] deep and well wooded," downstream from the present town of Glendale. Cow Creek is a major tributary of the South Umpqua River. The brigade apparently descended Cow Creek a short distance (possibly as far as Brandt siding). Ogden's Indian guide probably led the brigade on an almost "beeline"-straight route to the west-northwest—no matter what the intervening obstacles—toward the "large River" that promised beaver—the Middle Fork of the Coquille. Ogden remained at this location on Cow Creek for the following three days, losing his original guide and gaining another. On March 20 the brigade descended Cow Creek some distance.

MARCH 17: . . . *those who descended the Stream from the cut Rocks were obliged to return and those who ascended the Stream so far as they have seen report favourably ≤ Beaver not numerous still there are a few . . . we shall however remain here for two or three days and collect what we can for since our leaving the upper part of the Clammitte River the fur of the Beaver is certainly very indifferent here however they are far superior to any I have yet seen and it is generally the case those taken in small Streams are far superior.*

MARCH 18:—*yesterday our Guide expressing a wish to go in quest of Indians I consented at the same time sent a young man with him but he managed to escape from him . . . but in my opinion we can almost do without one now for one of the Trappers secured an old man and brought him to the Camp and from him we obtained all the information we required . . . one [of the Indians Ogden met this day] volunteered to accompany us and to guide us to the large River . . . miserable looking wretches . . . suprising to see them in this state being in a Country abounding in Deer . . . not one has even a Bow & Arrow to defend himself.*

MARCH 20: . . . *the fellow feels pleased to accompany us ≤ he is well warn'd he will when we reach the River be rewarded . . .—we did not start before 11 A.M. . . . we descended the Stream untill 4 P.M. when our Guide informed us we were to leave it and take a different route with a mountain to cross ≤ we encamped at the same time the Trappers started to examine the remainder of the Stream ≤ but from its now rapid descent altho wide and well wooded there is no appearance of Beaver. We had a good road and but few hills ≤ however from what we can see in advance I am not of opinion we shall be so fortunate tomorrow. Course this day North West.*

Although the chief trader gave no mileage figure for his travels on the 20th of March, he probably journeyed down Cow Creek (now a "wide and well wooded" stream, more deserving of the title "river" than "creek") about nine miles, crossing and recrossing the stream to avoid sections of steep banks. This would put the brigade's camp near the mouth of Darby Creek (a short distance above the present Cow Creek railroad siding). It is near this point that Cow Creek begins to make its sweeping turn from northwest to northeast. The trappers' previous complaint about "cut Rocks" along this stretch of Cow Creek undoubtedly referred both to the creek's rocky channel and to the trail along the stream. Cow Creek, from "Brandt" siding to well below Darby Creek, flows through a steep, 1,000-foot deep canyon, but a bank of level ground along the length of the stream would have been just sufficiently wide enough to allow the brigade to travel downstream without major difficulty. Although this was not a particularly difficult trek, Ogden looked with misgiving at the steep climb that the next day's journey would entail.

MARCH 21: . . . *it is full time for us to leave the Stream and seek another* ≲ *at ten we started turning our backs to the River and taking a due West Course* ≲ *we had not advanced fifty yards when we were surrounded by strong woods and our progress was*

March 20: we descended the Stream [Cow Creek] untill
4 P.M. when our Guide informed us we were to leave it and
take a different route with a mountain to cross.
March 21: at ten we started turning our backs to the River and
taking a due West Course ≲ *we had not advanced fifty yards*
when we were surrounded by strong woods and our progress
was slow. . . . steeper Hills cannot be found.

This downstream view of the Cow Creek canyon (near the mouth of Darby Creek) shows the steep, heavily timbered slopes (left) up which Ogden's men laboriously fought their way toward Big Dutchman Butte and the Middle Fork of the Coquille River. (Photo by author)

slow as we were obliged to have recourse to our axes, four men with me took the lead and we certainly found full employment ≤ our guide informed me it was impossible for us to cross the Mountain with Horses and some of the men proposed that I should not raise Camp and they would go in advance and make a road ≤ but to this I would not consent. . . . I have latterly within the last three years cross'd and recross'd Mountains but have not before this day had so many impediments to overcome ≤ steeper Hills cannot be found ≤ this with the cut Rocks we were obliged to throw our Horses down a most laborious task and also a most dangerous one . . . it is to me almost surprising they were not all kill'd. At five in the evening finding a small Stream and no appearance of a level Country before us we encamped . . . to console us our Guide promises we shall reach the River Tomorrow. . . . Distance this day nine miles.

March 21 was obviously one of Ogden's most trying days. No doubt his temper was short that evening as he wrote in his journal; seven hours of trail-clearing and urging the heavily-laden horses up through the "brush" no doubt had its effect on the chief trader's disposition. Based on its presumed departure from Cow Creek "due West," the brigade would have struggled up the densely forested, thirty to sixty percent slopes of the canyon. Cutting their way through the tangled undergrowth, Ogden and his trappers probably followed the west-trending ridges (across open outcrops of Umpqua Formation sandstone, the "cut Rocks") between Darby Creek and Union Creek to near the summit of Big Dutchman Butte. They would have crossed the divide just east of the peak, leaving the Umpqua River drainage and entering into the watershed of the Middle Fork of the Coquille. The "small Stream" the exhausted party chose to camp on most likely was the upper reaches of Dice Creek, a tributary of Twelvemile Creek.[55]

The 1961 edition (p.98, n.1) has Ogden leaving Allen Creek in Josephine County, and coming down into the "Rogue Valley" at Grants Pass. Even if one were to consider the 1961 version of the route correct to this point, this location cannot correlate with Ogden's preceding week of travel.

MARCH 22: . . . *At 7 A.M. we started, Course West following the small Stream which as the Country began to open was soon a large one and at 11 A.M. we reached a level Country and shortly after a fine large River, this is the Stream the natives have so often informed us was full of Beaver . . . the Trappers . . . so far as they descended the Stream saw not the slightest vestige of Beaver, those who ascended it found one Lodge and a dozen of Traps were sett . . . The Trappers after their trouble in the mountains are now vexed to find themselves disappointed . . . our expectations were certainly raised . . . but before we condem this Stream we must give it a trial. Our road this day altho far from being good was certainly far superior to yesterday ≤ still our Axes were made use off [of] and without we could not have advanced. Course West ≤ Dist. 8 Miles.*

Peter Ogden, by now possibly feeling like Coronado in quest of Gran Quivira, had at last reached the natives' fabled beaver-rich river—and found it to fall far short of his expectations. The 1961 edition places him at Grants Pass, but Ogden actually must have been on the Middle Fork of the Coquille, at or near the mouth of Twelvemile Creek (about ten miles east of the community of Remote). The brigade, using hatchets to clear a trail, descended Twelvemile Creek to the Coquille. Upon initial inspection, the river proved to be very disappointing. By this time, after several months of grumbling, Odgen's Freemen may have been on the verge of desertion. Most of the streams they had trapped since leaving the Bear Creek Valley had provided dismal returns, and the men desperately wanted to return south.

MARCH 23: . . . *six men started to examine the upper part of this River. . . . our guide went in quest of Indians and retd. with three ≦ from those we learn that the Umpqua Chief had visited this quarter with six Trappers from the Williamette and had taken all the Beaver . . . they also inform us these waters have no communication with the Umpqua but all discharge into the Clammitte River and to reach the former River we have yet a Mountain to cross and the distance is yet six days march . . . we all well know two [too] much stress cannot be placed on their reports*

MARCH 24: . . . *the six men that started yesterday arrived with 10 Beavers ≦ report a Rocky and Mountainous Contry . . . they advanced some distance but from the Cut Rocks could not proceed farther without making rafts and constantly crossing and recrossing the River ≦ its sources might be reached but otherwise impossible ≦ the cause prevented us from Trapping the sources of the River we left on the other side of the Mountains [the Rogue] . . . I am also of opinion both these Forks must take their rise in the vicinity of Sasty River . . . I have come to the determination of leaving Gervais with four men to Trap these Rivers and from thence endeavor to reach the Umpqua Country so as to open a communication between this quarter and Fort Vancouver which ought to have been affected many years since.*

During his two days on the Coquille, Ogden received word from the local Indians that the "Umpqua Chief" (most likely Alexander McLeod, chief trader of the HBC "Umpqua Brigade") had only recently trapped this river with six men. This particular account provides virtually certain evidence that Ogden was then in the Coquille (McLeod's "Shequits") River drainage, an area that had been thoroughly trapped by McLeod's men during the winter of 1826–27.[56] The six men Ogden had sent upstream returned with tales of the river's steep rocky canyon. This group apparently ascended the Middle Fork of the Coquille some distance along its rugged upper course, but they evidently did not go so far east as to reach the broad, open Camas Valley, where the Middle Fork winds along as a far gentler stream. Or, if in fact these six men actually did reach Camas Valley, they may have misrepresented the area's physical character so as to discourage the chief trader from further exploration in that direction. Their poor take of beaver from the trapped-out Coquille, combined with the trappers' knowledge of Ogden's propensity to explore every major valley and stream he learned of, may have led the men purposely to deceive their leader—that is, to describe the upper Middle Fork as not worth any further trouble. The puzzling reference to the Coquille being a tributary of the "Clammitte" was certainly the result of misunderstanding, linquistic or geographic, between Ogden and his Indian informants. Before leaving the Coquille, Ogden decided to have Jean Baptiste Gervais and four others remain behind. They were to work their way north to the Willamette and Fort Vancouver.[57]

On to the South Umpqua and back to the Klamath River

THE FIRST PART of this section, from the Middle Fork of the Coquille to the South Umpqua and back to the Rogue River, is often more confusing than the previous portion of Ogden's route. Although the exact route may be undecipherable, it is evident that Ogden returned to Cow Creek and crossed to the east side of the stream (probably near the point where he first reached it on March 26) over one of the numerous shallow cascades and fords in the vicinity of Darby Creek. Travelling down Cow Creek, Ogden would have realized later that day that the brigade must recross it in order to follow the course of the "large River" (the South Umpqua) that according to his guide and scouts, lay a short distance ahead of them. After recrossing Cow Creek by canoe, the brigade followed down the left bank of the Umpqua almost as far as Myrtle Creek. Discovering abundant signs of previous HBC trappers, Ogden returned up the South Umpqua, past the mouth of Cow Creek, to the vicinity of Days Creek.

After learning that the mountains south of the Days Creek camp were too steep to cross, Ogden decided to abandon the attempt to regain the "Sasty" (Rogue) via a direct southward march from Days Creek. The group quickly retraced its path down the South Umpqua and then up Cow Creek, returning to and recrossing the Rogue near Grants Pass. Endeavoring to explore the unseen river he had surmised to be the Klamath, the chief trader crossed the low range of hills south of Grants Pass and reached the Applegate River. He soon must have realized that this stream was not the "Clammitte," and sent some of his men to explore its upper reaches.

95

96

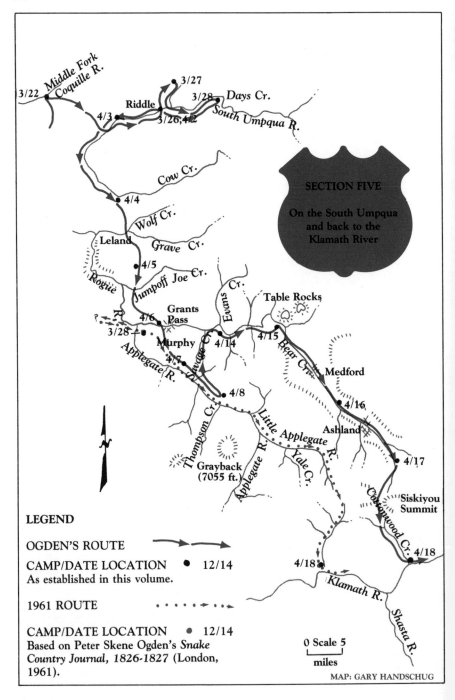

Middle Fork
Coquille R.

3/22
3/27
3/28
Days Cr.
Riddle
3/26,4/2
South Umpqua R.
4/3

Cow Cr.

4/4

SECTION FIVE

On the South Umpqua
and back to the
Klamath River

Wolf Cr.

Leland
Grave Cr.

4/5
Jumpoff Joe Cr.

Evans Cr.
Table Rocks

Rogue R.

Grants
Pass

4/6

3/28
Murphy
4/14
4/15

Applegate R.
4/7
Bear Cr.
Medford

4/8
4/16

Thompson Cr.
Little Applegate R.
Ashland

Grayback
(7055 ft.)
Applegate R.
Yale Cr.
4/17

Siskiyou
Summit

Cottonwood Cr.
4/18

LEGEND

OGDEN'S ROUTE ⟶

CAMP/DATE LOCATION ● 12/14
As established in this volume.

4/18
Klamath R.

1961 ROUTE •••••▸•▸

CAMP/DATE LOCATION ● 12/14
Based on Peter Skene Ogden's *Snake
Country Journal*, 1826-1827 (London,
1961).

Shasta R.

0 Scale 5
⊢————⊣
miles

MAP: GARY HANDSCHUG

Returning over the intervening hills to the "Sasty," at a point near the mouth of Evans Creek, the brigade followed the earlier trail back to the Bear Creek Valley and over the Siskiyou Mountains.

MARCH 26 [1827]: . . . at 9 A.M. we started and separated from Gervais & party ≤ I gave them orders not to abandon the Country ere they had examined & trapped all the streams they should find. . . . We cross'd over a point of Land and soon reached the River we were encamped on prior to our crossing the Mountains ≤ we followed it down to near its discharge in the large River in hopes of finding a fording place but could not ≤ we however found a Canoe and commenced crossing over and in the evening all [the pelts and supplies] was safe across. Dist. this day 6 miles ≤ Course North. This Stream [Cow Creek] has been examined almost from end to end and with the exception of those taken by us in the upper part has yielded nothing. . . . Trappers report they saw seven Bears ≤ from the number of tracks I have lately seen I believe them to be numerous in this quarter, it is a fine Country for them Acorns being most abundant and Roots also.

This is a particulary enigmatic entry. It puts the itinerary of the succeeding two weeks into confusion, and some "imaginative" editorial interpretation becomes necessary for the entries between March 26 and April 4. Ogden's actual route for this brief period remains "tenuous," but by a process of elimination his travels can be retraced in a general way.

The 1961 edition (p. 100, n. 1) states that the "River" the brigade "soon reached" this day was the Applegate; it must instead have been Cow Creek, somewhere downstream from the mouth of Darby Creek. Having left Gervais to trap his way north to the Willamette and Fort Vancouver, Ogden "cross'd over a point of Land" and reached "the River we were encamped on prior to our crossing the Mountains."[58] The brigade, by then familiar with the countryside, may have shortened the return trip by travelling easterly up one of the Coquille tributaries east of Twelvemile Creek.

Although Ogden failed specifically to mention the fact, his remarks in both this and the next day's entries make it apparent that soon after reaching Cow Creek the brigade crossed to its right bank (the east side) before descending it much further. One can offer at least two possible reasons for this: (1) Ogden wished to avoid the treacherously narrow footing visible to him along this stretch of the left bank, or (2) he hoped that the right bank would prove to be a better route once the party reached the lower reaches of Cow Creek. In the vicinity of Cow Creek siding there are several fording places, any of which Ogden could have used to cross from the west to the east side. However, a few miles below this point Cow Creek widens and deepens considerably; as mentioned previously it here becomes more deserving of the term "river" than "creek." As the trappers neared Cow Creek's confluence with the South Umpqua River, Ogden would have realized that they would have to *recross* Cow Creek, back to the left bank, so that they could descend the new "large River," the South Umpqua. This they did somewhere in the vicinity of the present town of Riddle, ferrying their goods across by means of an abandoned canoe. Ogden's course along Cow Creek would have been northeast, not north. His brief description of the countryside (good "Beaver country," abundant oaks) would certainly fit the valley of lower Cow Creek. The brigade probably camped within or near the site of Riddle, less than two miles above the South Umpqua River.

> MARCH 27: . . . At 7 A.M. we started ≤ cross'd over a long point and reached the main Stream ≤ we descended it for six miles and encamped on a fine large River and I may add covered with white Clover. In all my travels I have not yet seen a finer Country for Pasture than we have travelled over for some time past . . . consequently our Horses are certainly in prime order. This is certainly a fine Stream equal in size to the Sasty River and altho dead water and well wooded no appearance of many Beaver . . . It was 11 A.M. when we encamped and the Trappers started with their Traps to examine the lower part of the River and retd. late in the evening with all their Traps and reported we had not advanced far when from the cut Rocks it was impossible to follow the Stream and in Crossing over a point to avoid these Rocks we discouvered a large track made by [other] Trappers and from appearances the party not small ≤ as far as they judge from twenty to thirty Horses, they also saw in many places where Traps had been sett ≤ also one of the Hunters an Iroquois informed me he discouvered a Mountain which appeared to be known to him as being in the vicinity of the Umpqua Country, now I can not see what good can result from my following the track of this party . . . tomorrow without loss of time I shall return my steps and endeavour to reach the Clammette River ≤ but we must procure a Guide if we do not wish to return by the route we came and this I certainly would wish to avoid. . . . Course North East.

Leaving the lower Cow Creek encampment, Ogden's group travelled over the low range of hills just northeast of Riddle and soon reached the left bank of the South Umpqua River. The party descended the South Umpqua for several miles to the northeast, encountering the relatively wide stretch of flat valley land later known as Missouri Bottom. This was an easy half-day's travel. Ogden sang the new river's praises: it was a "fine Stream," comparable in size to the Sasty (Rogue), but he was puzzled by the lack of beaver in its deep, quiet waters. The adjacent land was richly endowed with "white Clover" and other "Pasture" cover. Because Ogden encamped so early (probably at a site less than a mile upstream from the present Southern Pacific Railroad siding of Weaver), his trappers eagerly continued downstream. They returned that evening, dejected after reaching "cut Rocks" a short distance below the main camp. The men had been forced to cross over a "point" away from the river. This point almost certainly would have been the South Umpqua's narrow gorge at the mouth of

March 27: we started ≦ cross'd over a long point and reached the main Stream ≦ we descended it for six miles and encamped on a fine large River and I may add covered with white Clover. . . . This is certainly a fine Stream equal in size to the Sasty ["Sastise," or Rogue] River.

After returning over the steep divide between the Coquille River and Cow Creek, the brigade followed Cow Creek down to its confluence with the South Umpqua River (here situated across the center of the photograph at the base of the hills). The wide alluvial terrace is known as Missouri Bottom, located a short distance north of the town of Riddle. The brigade would have passed, left-to-right, along the far shore of the river, camping near the base of the bluffs seen at the right edge of the photograph. (Photo by author)

Myrtle Creek, virtually impossible for horse travel along the left bank. From this barrier the trappers must have turned northwest, away from the river, and crossed the steep ridge that lies between Sheep Hill on the west and the river on the east. From this summit they would have quickly regained the left bank of the South Umpqua. Somewhere near this spot Ogden's men discovered the "large track made by Trappers," as well as abundant evidence that the river had been cleaned of beaver. Again, Ogden's party had come upon the recent trail of McLeod's "Umpqua Brigade," probably left by the Depaty-Laframboise group during its southward march. To confirm this interpetation, one of Ogden's Iroquois "Hunters" asserted that he had just "discouvered a Mountain which appeared to be

March 27: the Trappers started . . . to examine the lower part of the [South Umpqua] River . . . and reported we had not advanced far when from the cut Rocks it was impossible to follow the Stream and in Crossing over a point to avoid these Rocks we discovered a large track made by [other] Trappers.

This westward view shows the point where the South Umpqua (flowing along the base of the hill on the left) enters a narrow canyon (center-right) at Myrtle Creek. The "point" over which Ogden's men crossed was probably the hill on the left. On the other side they found the tracks of Alexander McLeod's "Umpqua Brigade." (Photo by author)

---

known to him as being in the vicinty of the Umpqua Country." Thus, having encountered the "Umpqua Brigade's" trail only a short distance from its Lookingglass Valley basecamp, Peter Ogden had closed the loop in the exploration of the major river systems of southwest Oregon—and the myth of the great "Buonaventura River" thereby shrank considerably.

The chief trader saw no sense in tarrying along another trapped-out river. Ogden could now in good conscience finally "return . . . [his] steps and endeavor to reach the Clammette River." But true to his adventurous character, his intention was to follow a *different* return route if at all possible.

MARCH 28: . . . *It was 9 A.M. ere we started . . . Being anxious about procuring a Guide I gave orders to the Trappers on reaching the Fork [the confluence of Cow Creek and the South Umpqua] to ascend it beyond our encampment of the 26th or as far as they could or the Country permit. I then started with a man in pursuit of Indians . . . all the information we could obtain from them does not give us great encouragement to proceed in the direction we propose going in. At 3 P.M. I rejoined the Camp who were encamped in the vicinity of the Mountain. Course in ascending the Fork North West [mis-copy for "North East"] ≤ Dist. this day 15 miles—with the exception of Climate which is at this season is very rainy this is certainly a fine Country ≤ the soil is from the variety of flowers grass Clover and trees of all kinds very rich and by culture no doubt would produce well, . . . from the number of new Graves I have seen lately I am of opinion starvation has been the cause of their [the Indians'] death. . . . in conversing with four elderly men this day I could obtain no information of the Country ≤ between this and the Clammette River as far as the eye could reach from a very high Hill it appears to me to be a most Mountainous Country and without a Guide to cross over the Country I shall not attempt it but follow up this Stream untill we reach our old track, we shall have the Mountain to cross or at least part of it and we must hope it will prove better than in the direction we crossed it ≤ we shall also be enabled to examine the remainder of this Stream.*

There is no major stream anywhere in the region that one would "ascend" in a northwestern direction. Ogden's stated course of "North West" is certainly either his or the Fort Vancouver clerk's copy-error for "North East," the direction in which he and his men would have ascended the South Umpqua River from its "Fork" with Cow Creek. Typically, Ogden made no mention of his course direction for the backtrack portion of this day's travel.

Ogden sent his men ahead with instructions "on reaching the Fork" (of Cow Creek and the South Umpqua) to ascend the main stream (the Umpqua) beyond their Riddle encampment. This would have involved crossing Cow Creek again. They travelled about fifteen miles upstream, passing just north of the site of Canyonville, and probably stopped in the vicinity of Days Creek. Ogden, unsuccessful in his effort to find new guides, joined his trappers later in the afternoon. Climbing a "very high Hill" (Beal Mountain?), he remarked on the mountainous country visible to the south. The forbidding terrain evidently caused Ogden to consider continuing up the South Umpqua and crossing the crest of the Cascades ("the Mountain") to the upper Klamath Basin.[59] The next day he dispatched a scout upriver to see if this idea was practical.

MARCH 29: . . . *At day light I sent a man with orders to proceed up the Stream to ascertain if there be a possibility of our advancing in that direction ≤ in the evening late he arrived and informed me it was impossible, for one encampt. the road was good farther the reverse ≶ he compares our track across the Mountain [Cow Creek-Coquille divide] as a good road compared to where he has been and says neither man or Horse can pass consequently we need not attempt it ≶ I do not at all feel inclined to return by the road we came altho I am truly anxious to be out of this Country.*

This upstream view of the South Umpqua is near Days Creek, the farthest east that Ogden ascended that river. One of his scouts, however, may have travelled beyond South Umpqua Falls before returning to Ogden's Days Creek camp with discouraging news about the upper river's steep canyon. From this point, Ogden retraced his steps back to the Rogue River. (Photo by author)

Ogden's scout probably ascended the river well above South Umpqua Falls, where the steep, heavily forested river canyon, with its numerous sheer-faced basalt cliffs, would have impeded his travel. Stubbornly refusing to accept defeat, Ogden then sent two more men to reconnoiter a possible route over the rugged range just to the south:

MARCH 30: . . . *at the break of day I sent two men to discouver a road in another direction and if we fail there also there is no alternative for us but again take the old track ≤ the very idea of this vexes me . . . Since I have been here I have observed the Natives from the dawn of the day untill late in the evening employed in digging Roots and the greter [greater] part of the night is spent in pounding and preparing their food nor do they appear to collect more than a sufficiency in one days labour than one meal.* ·

APRIL 1: . . . *at mid day the two men arrived and the report they bring coincides with the Natives that is it is impossible ≤ it is as far as they proceeded one continued Mountain of Rocks and strong woods ≤ they left their Horses and endeavored to reach the height of Land but from the impediments they met with their progress was so slow they abandoned any farther attempt and retd. . . . . there is now [no] alternative left but to return by the road we came.*

The two scouts probably ascended south up Shively Créek or some other nearby tributary of the South Umpqua. They would have encountered the dense, often brush-choked, conifer forest of the steep, north-aspect slopes, and turned back after a day's hard going.

APRIL 2: . . . *We were detained three hours at the crossing place but continued on untill the evening when we reached the foot of the Mountains from whence Gervais and party separated from us.*

This is the first in a series of very terse entries. The brigade descended the South Umpqua and again must have crossed to the left bank of Cow Creek (probably camping at their previous bivouac near Riddle). Ogden referred to the "Mountains from whence Gervais . . . separated from us"—the Cow Creek-Coquille divide. For the next three days, Ogden beat a hasty retreat towards the Rogue. Following his old track, the chief trader was very sparing of detail, including course directions and distances.

APRIL 3: . . . *at 6 A.M. we started and at 3 P.M. we had the Mountains in our rear and glad was I to see it so . . . On our arrival here we saw a few Indians in the Plains at their daily labour.*

This entry evidently referred to the Takelma or Umpqua Indians gathering roots from some of the open, oak woodland areas—locally and historically refered to as "balds" ("Plains").

APRIL 4: . . . *At 10 AM we started and at 2 PM we reached our encampment ≤ it was here we took upwards of 80 Beaver consequently cannot expect any more. . . . four Trappers started in advance ≤ the remainder will start tomorrow and proceed direct for the main Stream. . . .*

APRIL 5: . . . *at six A.M. we started ≤ weather fine and clear ≤ we found the road good . . . I was determined to push on and did not encamp before sun sett when we reached our first encampment leaving Sasty River ≤ what with the Mountains & Hills and distance our Horses were certainly low.*

April 5 was a long day's journey—a forced march of at least twenty miles, possibly from upper Cow Creek, or from at least Grave Creek, south to Jumpoff Joe Creek near Merlin. This had been up to two days' travel on the brigade's north-bound trek. Ogden began the next day by leaving his old path, intending to visit the "Clammette" (actually the Applegate River) by taking a detour to the southwet. His advance trappers quickly returned and dissuaded him from this approach. Thinking they had reached the Clammette, these men had reached the Rogue River (the "main Stream" referred to in the April 4 entry) somewhere northwest of Merlin. They undoubtedly descended it some distance, entering the steep Hellgate Canyon of the lower Rogue. They rejoined their leader with tales of "cut Rocks and Mountains," and Ogden then redirected the party's travel to the south-southeast. They soon reached their original "Sasty River" crossing near Grants Pass:

APRIL 6: . . . *at 6 A.M. we started and left our old track taking a South west course with the intention of reaching the Clammitte River but at 10 A.M. I met all the Trappers on their return who from the cut Rocks and Mountains after descending a considerable distance down the Stream had been obliged to return . . . it now appears to me from what I have seen and from the information I have obtained from the Natives that the Clammitte River forms a junction with the large Stream we saw the tracks of Ft. Vancouver party [Coquille or South Umpqua] ≤ it certainly takes its course through the same range of Mountains we have been travelling over . . . I see no good that would result from our attempting to force a passage down as the party alluded [to] [McLeod's brigade] have already examined the lower part ≤ if not it can easily be affected either by the Coast or Umpqua River [the North Umpqua]. . . . proceeded on untill five in the evening when we reached our crossing place at the Sasty River ≤ here we soon found a Canoe and the Trappers lost no time in crossing.*

Most of the brigade crossed to the south side of the Rogue River that same evening. Ogden's rather lengthy discussion of the "Clammitte River" here shows that he still regarded the as-yet unseen (by him) Applegate River (and, therefore, also the Rogue below its confluence with the Applegate) to be the Klamath River. Further, he believed that virtually all of the major streams he had seen over the past two months were tributaries of the "Clammitte." In short, Ogden surmised that all of the rivers they had seen since leaving the lava beds of northeast California were part of a single, huge drainage system, a misconception that would be perpetuated on the Arrowsmith map several years later.[60] The next day Ogden determined to reach the so-called Clammitte *above* its juncture with the "Sasty":

APRIL 7: *At 8 A.M. this morning all was safe across and the Trappers started in advance with their Traps . . . on starting the River making a considerable bend we cross'd over a long point and at 12 we reached the Clammette River and advanced only a short distance . . . Dist. 9 miles ≦ Course South East.*

Less than half a day's travel south from the Rogue crossing brought the party across a "long point" (probably over the gentle Allen Creek-Onion Creek divide, along the route of present Oregon Highway 238) to the north bank of the Applegate River. The trappers would have reached the Applegate, which Ogden this day persisted in referring to as the "Clam-

---

April 7: At 8 *A.M.* this morning all was safe across [the Rogue] . . . we cross'd over a long point and at 12 we reached the Clammette River.

As Ogden would soon realize, it was not the "Clammette," but a much smaller river (the Applegate). This view near Murphy, south of the city of Grants Pass, is at or near the spot where Ogden first would have seen the Applegate. (Photo by author)

mette," at or near the present town of Murphy. They probably camped near the mouth of Board Shanty Creek. This was the last time that Ogden used the name "Clammette" for this stream. If he had had any initial doubts about this river's identity (for example, due to the Applegate's narrower channel), the explorations by his men during the next four days confirmed them. Their upstream reconnaissance of the Applegate made it plain that Ogden was on an entirely different river, one with a far smaller drainage area than the Klamath.

APRIL 8: At 6 A.M. we started with the hopes of joining our Trappers but at 10 A.M. the rain again obliged us to encamp. . . . An Indian it is supposed stole a Trap but from the dry Grass and Stones his track could not be followed. Distance this day 8 miles ≦ stony road but not hilly ≦ Course East.

Ogden's trappers had scattered upon reaching the Applegate. It seems likely that Murphy Creek and Williams Creek were among the tributary streams they explored; the Applegate River would not have been too difficult for them to cross. This day Ogden advanced "East" (actually southeast), up the Applegate. He probably reached a point opposite the mouth of Thompson Creek (at the present community of Applegate). This was the farthest upstream that Ogden himself travelled in the Applegate Valley. The "stony road" must have referred to the numerous gravel bars and rock outcrops along the north bank of the Applegate. The nearly level floor of the Applegate Valley here is nearly half a mile in width.

APRIL 9: . . . here we are surrounded by high and lofty mountains and well covered with snow. At an early hour this morning I sent two men to proceed in ascending the Stream as far as the Mountains will allow them so as to advance farther in that direction ≦ if not we shall strike across and follow our old track.

The main party remained at the Thompson Creek area. Now aware that his course up the Applegate seemed to be leading the expedition into a blind alley, Ogden dispatched two scouts to go as far upstream as possible. The "high and lofty mountains" would have included Grayback Mountain and other peaks of the Siskiyous visible to the south. His statement "if not we shall strike across and follow our old track" of course means that he would return north to the "Sasty" and retrace his steps up that stream. This is, in fact, just what the brigade was soon forced to do.

APRIL 10: This morning I sent two men in a Southern direction to examine the Country in case of there being Streams which at present we are not aware off. Four Indians from the lower part of the River paid us a visit ≦ all the information I could obtain from them was that they were ignorant of any other River but the one we are now encamped on ≦ as far as they know one continued Mountain and at any season with Horses impossible to cross and at present from the depth of Snow no one can cross. The men that started yesterday with their Traps retd. ≦ no success ≦ report they *reached the Mountain ≶ the River on both sides well lin'd with Stones and the water remarkable clear.*

Two more scouts were sent out this day, probably up Thompson Creek (in a "Southern direction"). Meanwhile the two men previously sent out returned from their abortive exploration up the Applegate. They would have ascended the river southward, well above Ruch, probably reaching the river canyon beyond present Applegate Lake reservoir. The "Four Indians" most likely were Athapascan-speaking Dakubetede. These people inhabited the Applegate Valley and would have been familiar with the deep snowpack in the high-elevation headwaters of the river. They discouraged Ogden from attempting to cross the Siskiyous via the upper Applegate River.

April 9: we are surrounded by high and lofty mountains.
April 10: This morning I sent two men in a Southern direction to examine the Country.
April 11: their progress soon arrested by mountains ≶ one they ascended and found on an average four feet of Snow.

This southward view across the Applegate Valley (the Applegate River's course is from left-to-right, across the center of the photograph) shows the Thompson Creek drainage in the distance. Ogden camped somewhere along the river near here while his scouts evidently ascended the deadend canyons of both the main Applegate and Thompson Creek. The men may have climbed the snowy slopes of 7,000-foot Grayback Mountain, visible on the right horizon. (Photo by author)

APRIL 11: . . . *the men that started yesterday are retd. No appearance of any Stream in the direction they have been ≤ their progress soon arrested by Mountains one they ascended and found on an average four feet of Snow. I now feel more than ever anxious to leave this Country being now more than ever firmly of opinion it is not a Beaver one nor was it ever intended it should be one. A dozen Indians paid us a visit . . . the information they give of the Country to the Southward corresponds with the account the men bring.*

The final pair of scouts returned, probably having travelled up Thompson Creek and then perhaps into the headwaters of Carberry Creek (one of the upper Applegate's main tributaries). They may have climbed up the slopes of Grayback Mountain, Big Sugarloaf or some other nearby peak until their ascent was blocked by snow. Finally giving up on his tenacious search for a new route, Ogden wrote disparagingly of the Applegate Valley and returned north. However, nearly fifty of the brigade's horses were run off by wolves, stalling the group's return to the Rogue for an additional two days. All of the horses were found unharmed (several of them having followed the trail back to the Rogue), and Ogden left the Applegate Valley on April 14.

APRIL 14: *At 7 A.M. we started ≤ cross'd over a long point [probably the Miners Creek-Savage Creek divide] and at 10 A.M. we reached the Sasty River ≤ proceeded on in ascending the Stream untill we reached our encampment of the 5th ultimo . . . the water has fallen 6 feet perpendicular ≤ it is still however a bold Stream and also a very strong one and both sides of the River well lin'd with Rocks and Stones ≤ these from the state of the water did not appear when we passed here.*

Returning to the Rogue near the mouth of Savage Creek, Ogden ascended the river to his March 5–6 encampmenth opposite the mouth of Evans Creek. He remarked on how much the Sasty's water level had fallen, but stated that it remained a substantial river.

APRIL 15: . . . *at 8 A.M. the rain ceased and at 10 we started ≤ fair weather was of short duration when rain again commenced ≤ we however reached our encampment and it appearing likely to continue and our furs exposed I encamped.*

Following the Rogue back upstream, this evening Ogden probably camped near the prior site, below the mouth of Bear Creek (again, somewhere in sight of the Table Rocks). Ogden's journal comments for this by-now-familiar territory were very curt; they provide little or no additional geographic description.

APRIL 16: *Started early . . . late in the day reached the encampment where our Horses were wounded and kill'd ≤ the roads far superior to when we last travell'd here.*

Following their February trail back up the Bear Creek Valley, the trappers reached their February "11–15" [10–14] encampment near the mouth of Wagner Creek.

APRIL 17: *This morning on rising we found the ground covered with Snow . . . we however started but at 2 P.M. the storm was so violent we were glad to encamp ≤ I had hopes of crossing the Mountains this day but have been disappointed ≤ there is every appearance we shall have Snow to encounter in crossing.*

A late, spring snowstorm prevented Ogden from crossing the Siskiyous this day. The brigade would have stopped somewhere along Emigrant Creek or lower Hill Creek.

APRIL 18: *Snow again in the night ≤ from our Horses being far scattered we did not start before 9 A.M. ≤ cross'd the Mountains with ease there not being more than a foot of snow in any part, we continued on untill 5 P.M. when we reached the Clammette River and encamped.*

The brigade's second crossing of Siskiyou Summit proved to be easier than their north-bound traverse had been. They rapidly descended along Cottonwood Creek and reached the Klamath River late that afternoon. Ogden noted his eagerness to learn the whereabouts of McKay's party.[61] The chief trader was now anxious to turn his course towards home.

SECTION SIX:
Klamath River to Tule Lake and the upper Pit River

T HIS IS THE FINAL SECTION of Ogden's route that is in doubt. The 1961 edition implies that Ogden simply retraced his previous trail, but the chief trader's journal indicates that some straightening and shortening of the earlier route occurred, especially in the vicinity of Lost River. In brief, Ogden followed up the Klamath River to the vicinity of Long Prairie Creek and headed cross-country over the Pokegema Plateau. He returned to the Klamath and again crossed it at his original location a short distance below Klamath Falls. From his crossing-point, Ogden headed east to the Lost River and descended it a short distance before crossing to its northeast bank. From Lost River, the brigade reached the southeast corner of Tule Lake and then continued southeast over the low divide that separates the Lost River drainage from that of Pit River. The trappers would have reached Pit River via either Turner Creek or Howards Gulch.

APRIL 19 [1827]: . . . wonderfull accounts of Mr. McKays success [given by the Indians]. . . .

APRIL 20: . . . we started at 7 A.M. and at 2 P.M. we reached our encampment of 2nd [1st] Feb [back at Beaver Basin, present Copco Lake].

APRIL 21: . . . I must either wait the arrival of Mr. McKays news here or at the Clammitte Lake ≦ I shall remain here two or three days.

APRIL 22: . . . Late this afternoon I was rather suprised at Mr. McKays arrival. [McKay's take was 735 beaver and otter] . . . this number was taken in two small Streams that discharge in the Clammitte River both which they clear'd and were on

111

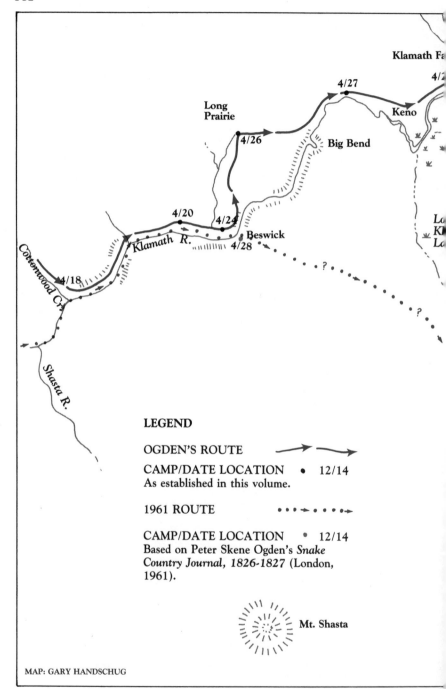

Klamath Fa

4/27

4/2

Long
Prairie

Keno

4/26

Big Bend

4/20

4/24

Beswick

Klamath R.

4/28

?

4/18

?

Cottonwood Cr.

Shasta R.

Lo
Kl
Lo

LEGEND

OGDEN'S ROUTE

CAMP/DATE LOCATION   •   12/14
As established in this volume.

1961 ROUTE

CAMP/DATE LOCATION   •   12/14
Based on Peter Skene Ogden's *Snake
Country Journal, 1826-1827* (London,
1961).

Mt. Shasta

MAP: GARY HANDSCHUG

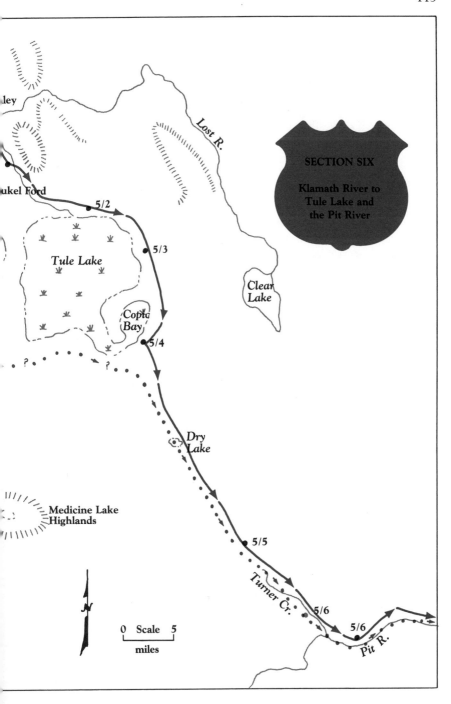

SECTION SIX

**Klamath River to
Tule Lake and
the Pit River**

Lost R.

ley

ukel Ford

5/2

Tule Lake

5/3

Clear
Lake

Copic
Bay

5/4

?   ?

Dry
Lake

Medicine Lake
Highlands

5/5

N

0   Scale   5

miles

Turner Cr.

5/6

5/6

Pit R.

their route to another reported to be a large one but from the deep Snows in the Mountains were obliged to abandon it in that direction.

McKay's harvest of pelts put Ogden's total tally well over the needed 1,500 mark. From Ogden's comments it is clear that McKay's party had spent the intervening two months trapping south of the Klamath River, most likely along the Shasta and Little Shasta rivers, and possibly the Scott River as well. The deep snows on the west flank of Mt. Shasta (near present Dunsmuir) evidently prevented them from reaching the Sacramento River, the "reported . . . large one."

APRIL 23: *It is almost incredible the flocks of Grey and White Geese that pass'd over.*

APRIL 24: . . . *we rais'd Camp starting at 7 A.M. and joined Mr. McKay's Party at 12 ≤ distance not more than four miles ≤ the roads from the rain of yesterday are certainly in a most horrid state and it was with difficulty in many places the Horses could extricate themselves out of the mud.*

Ogden and McKay joined forces this day, probably at or near the mouth of Long Prairie Creek. The muddy soils of the Klamath River canyon again tormented the brigade's horses. The following day, April 25, was spent in camp while McKay attempted to retrieve some stolen traps.

APRIL 26: . . . *we rais'd Camp leaving our old track in ascending the Stream in hopes of being enabled to sett a few Traps, in this we succeeded but to my regret as our Horses will feel the affects ≤ for upwards of two hours one continued Stone and it was painful to them ≤ on reaching our encampment of the 29th [28th] Jan'y we encamped.*

Ogden, in hopes of adding a few more beaver to his harvest of furs before leaving this productive stretch of the Klamath, entered the lower end of the gorge for a short distance before turning north and arriving at the January "25–30" [24–29] campsite at or near Long Prairie.

APRIL 27: . . . *we then started ≤ I had hopes of making two of our winter days journey but could not succeed from the low state of our Horses ≤ we shall however be enabled to reach our crossing place tomorrow. . . . as we advance I find vegetation very backward compared to the Country we have come from.*

The rapid, long distance travel of the past few weeks had taken its toll on the trappers' mounts. Instead of reaching the river crossing as he had hoped, Ogden apparently camped somewhere west of Keno, probably in the vicinity of Spencer Creek. Soon returning to the domain of sagebrush and juniper, he noted the changing vegetation.

APRIL 28: *We rais'd Camp, four men with their Traps remain here and will overtake us tomorrow. We started at 7 A.M. and reached the crossing place at 2 P.M. . . . here we found a small village containing a dozen Huts . . . 6 Dogs traded.*

April 26: we raised Camp leaving our old track in ascending the Stream [the Klamath] . . . on reaching our encampment of the 29th [28th] Jan'y we encamped.

Having retraced his route along the Klamath, Ogden returned to Long Prairie, the brigade's campsite of almost three months before. (Photo by author)

Ogden followed the Klamath upstream (although he no doubt short-ened his original trail) to the January crossing place just below Klamath Falls. The brigade remained on the right (west) bank through the next day to await the rear group of trappers.

APRIL 30: *With the assistance of two large Canoes we soon crossed all over the River safe . . . shortly after [we] started ≲ at mid day we reached the River seen by us on the 16th [15th] Decb. and followed down the stream untill 2 P.M. when we en-camped. Dist 18 miles.*

After ferrying the furs and supplies across the Klamath that morning, the party reached the Lost River somewhere near Henley and followed it downstream for some distance (probably at least past the site of Wilson Dam) before resting for the night. Ogden's distance of "18 miles" seems a bit inflated; he probably travelled no more than twelve to fifteen miles this day. The chief trader, hoping to procure a guide to the east, was pleased to learn that a "large Camp of Indians" lay along their path for the next day.

MAY 1: . . . *at 7 A.M. we started and at 12 we reached the Camp of Indians ≲ about 60 men all busily employed in fishing and appear to have a good stock of Carp collected but a most indifferent kind small and scarcely eatable.*

The group descended Lost River for several hours and then probably camped very near the Modoc fishing village of "Wa'isha."[62] This large, year-round village was situated at Stukel Ford, the only natural crossing (aside from the "Stone Bridge," a partially submerged basalt ledge located well downstream) along this section of the Lost River. Although Ogden failed to note having crossed the Lost River during this leg of the journey, he must have done so, and Stukel Ford (not Stone Bridge) would have been the most likely site.

On the morning of May 2, the brigade crossed the Lost River at Stukel Ford. This southeastward (downstream) view near the fording place shows the effects of modern irrigation diversions on the river's width and depth. Tule Lake Basin lies just beyond the horizon. (Photo by author)

MAY 2: *We succeeded this morning in securing two Guides . . . we advanced eight miles and encamped and later in the evening ≶ Mr. McKay with the Guides arrived.*

After crossing to the east side of Lost River at Stukel Ford, Ogden would have paralleled the left bank of the stream until reaching the vicinity of present-day Merrill. The evening's camp may have been south of Dodds Hollow and about one mile west of Adams Point.

MAY 3: *. . . We started at 8 A.M. following our last winters track untill 2 P.M. when we encamped on the border of a small Lake . . . the guides inform us we shall soon have a stony Country.*

The trappers rejoined their previous December-January trail once again, apparently following it to one of the small open patches of water on the northeast edge of Tule Lake.

MAY 4: *It was nine ere we were in readiness . . . we however reached late in the evening the encampment from whence I returned last winter and tomorrow our Guides will take the lead ≶ they inform us the River we are going to is far distant . . . Muschetoes troublesome last night.*

The "encampment from whence [I] returned last winter" must be the December "27" [26] and January "4" [3] camp at the east side of Copic Bay. It is unclear why this day's relatively easy journey should have taken so much time. From this point on, the brigade would be crossing unfamiliar territory and Ogden felt fortunate in having guides. The thirsty Tule Lake mosquitoes, at their height during this season, also raised comment from Ogden. Here he first mentioned the new river he intended to reach, the Pit River.

MAY 5: *At 7 A.M. we started our Guides warning us the distance was great ere we should find water . . . At 1 P.M. we reached a small bason of water formed by the melting of Snow from the mountain scarcely sufficient for our wants but the Guides thought it most prudent to encamp . . . we travelled over a barren Country at intervals wooded with Norway Pines ≶ Soil sandy ≶ Course South East Distance 18 miles. We did not see the track of a living creature nor does it appear to be a country inhabited by Indians as the track we followed in many places scarcely appeared.*

The brigade had this day travelled over much of the high desert southeast of Tule Lake. Widely scattered ponderosa pines do grow in this area, but it is largely sagebrush country. The trappers probably camped at or near McKay Flat (in the general vicinity of Hackamore). The "small bason of water" at which the party refreshed itself was possibly one of the several shallow, seasonal ponds located in this vicinity; these would have been along the brigade's route of travel.[63]

May 5: we travelled over a barren Country at intervals wooded with Norway Pines.

Ogden's path paralleled present California Highway 139. This westward view from the highway shows scattered ponderosa pine, with the Medicine Lake Highlands rising in the distance; the encroaching juniper forest was not present in Ogden's time. (Photo by author)

MAY 6: *at 8 A.M. we started ≤ we advanced three hours when we reached a fine looking River for Beaver well wooded and muddy banks . . . we had a good road ≤ wood scarce and the Country more open.*

Ogden reached the right bank of the narrow, meandering Pit River before noon, and he was definitely impressed with the beaver-potential of this headwater tributary of the Sacramento. His travel from McKay Flat most likely would have been down Turner Creek or Howards Gulch, putting him at the river near the present town of Canby. His trappers explored down the lower part and returned the next day with 42 beaver skins. Ogden commented on the local Achumawi Indians' practice of excavating deep pits in order to capture deer and other game. One of the

May 6: at 8 A.M. we started ≲ we advanced three hours when we reached a fine looking River for Beaver . . . wood scarce and the Country more open.

This southeastward view is of the narrow, meandering upper Pit River (center) near Canby, California. From here Ogden turned his course upstream (left) and headed to the river's source at Goose Lake, and then continued on across southeastern Oregon to the Snake River. (Photo by author)

---

brigade's horses fell into a trap and was fatally impaled on the sharp wooden stakes; Pit River now had a name.[64]

≲   ≲   ≲

From here, Ogden's "Snake Country Brigade" followed up the Pit River and eventually crossed the arid southeast quarter of Oregon to reach the Snake River on July 16—after ten months of travel, the first date they actually saw that river on the entire journey.

Sending his brigade on to Fort Nez Perce, near the confluence of the Snake and the Columbia rivers, Ogden returned to Fort Vancouver. There, the men were paid, the account books tallied, the furs baled, and the chief trader's dog-eared journal copied for shipment to the Company's Beaver House headquarters in London. Reporting, in the comparative luxury of Fort Vancouver, to Dr. John McLoughlin about his year's adventures—no doubt at least some of them were retold as after-dinner stories accompanied by a decanter of the Doctor's brandy—Peter Skene Ogden remained a busy man. Soon it would be time to set off again into unknown country as the leader of another Snake Country Brigade.

CONCLUSIONS

FOR DECADES Peter Skene Ogden's 1826–27 journal has been considered something of a puzzle. The document's supposed geographic confusion and vagueness made it a curious anomaly when compared to Ogden's other, apparently easier-to-follow journals. However, when the modern reader allows for certain original omissions and later mistakes in the journal's transcription, the 1826–27 route of travel becomes far easier to trace. In general terms, the chief trader's itinerary is not the enigma it formerly was thought to be. The foregoing reinterpretation of Ogden's travels makes some major geographic changes from the 1961 version of his route, and these changes permit a high degree of "fit" with the actual written account that Ogden left behind. This "new" version of the route may well be wrong in certain locations; future historians will no doubt refine and correct some of the details.

≶   ≶   ≶

"WHERE DID THE FIRST WHITE MEN *in the area actually pass? What streams did they follow and where did they camp?*" Within the larger historical theme of Pacific Northwest exploration, such site-specific questions have little significance. Yet, they are the sort that some historians love to debate. One may justifiably ask, "So what? Of what possible historical importance can this be?" after reading yet another version of a long-dead trapper's route of travel. In the case of Ogden's exploration of northern California and southwestern Oregon, its importance touches many areas. A correct interpretation of this 1826–27 route allows for inquiry into other histori-

121

cal topics such as territorial boundaries of local aboriginal groups at the time of Euro-American contact, origins of major geographic place-names, developments in early Pacific Northwest cartography, and the initial evolution of the region's most important north-south travel route.

Territorial Boundaries of the
Aboriginal Inhabitants

THE MAIN TESTIMONY for the location of aboriginal boundaries in northern California and southwestern Oregon is formed by less than a dozen ethnographic studies (most of them researched and published during the early twentieth century). Based largely on the accounts of then-elderly Indian informants who had been young children at the time of initial Euro-American contact, some of these sources contradict each other. Representatives of one native group would lay claim to a specific piece of territory while those of another group would just as emphatically claim it as theirs.[65] The result has been confusion over just what lands were included within the primary territorial limits of any particular Indian group. Since Ogden was the first person to observe and write about the local native populations, his journal provides crucial additional evidence for the correct placement of their boundaries.

The journal does not shed any light on the boundary between the Klamath (his "Clammitte") and the Modoc Indians. Ogden, in fact, made no distinction between them at all. This fact is not too surprising due to the close linguistic and cultural affinity of these two peoples. In any case, there has been relatively little ethnographic debate over their adjacent territorial claims. However, the question of Shasta-Klamath and Shasta-Takelma boundaries has been (and continues to be) much disputed, and it is here that Ogden proves helpful.

The approximate dividing line between the Penutian-speaking Klamath-Modoc Indians on the one hand and the Hokan-speaking Shasta varies considerably, depending upon which ethnographic source is consulted.[66] The 1961 version of Ogden's travels would seem to place the division somewhere near present Copco Lake, but it is now apparent that the relevant journal entries actually dealt with the easternmost portion of the Klamath River canyon. Based on all of Ogden's various references to the "Sastise" (between late December 1826 and early February 1827), it is virtually certain that the Shasta formerly resided along the Klamath River as far upstream as the Big Bend-Salt Caves area.[67] This precipitous canyon was the upper limit of most salmon runs, and it consequently would have formed a logical economic and physiographic border between the Shasta, with their riverine-focused economy, and the Klamath, who relied heavily on the resources of marshes and lakes. Nevertheless, it was a border over which (according to Ogden's mention of "Clammitte"-"Sastise" hostilities at or near here) there had been bloody disputes.[68] As a result of persistent Klamath-Modoc attacks during the Euro-American contact period, the upstream Shasta bands may have moved to the lower end of the canyon, near Beswick.

Ogden's account provides clear evidence that the Shasta did in fact inhabit the upper (southern) Bear Creek Valley.[69] Although it never mentions the Takelma by name, his journal also can be used to locate this group's approximate boundary with the Bear Creek band of the Shasta. Ethnographic accounts have located this line variously from as far north as the Jacksonville area to as far south as the crest of the Siskiyous. Ogden's journal entries for the second week of February, when the brigade travelled north from Siskiyou Summit to the Talent area make it plain that his "Sastise" guides became quite apprehensive about infringing on the territory of the "next Tribe" (probably the Upland Takelma's) territory and warned the chief trader to be on his guard.[70] The guides voiced their concern when the brigade reached the Wagner Creek-Talent area along upper Bear Creek. In addition, it was at this same location that several of Ogden's horses were shot with arrows, apparently by the unfriendly "next Tribe" and not by the to-date quite congenial Shasta. Therefore, the most probable Takelma-Shasta boundary at the time of Euro-American contact would have been somewhere between Ashland and Talent.[71]

Once he had passed beyond Takelma territory, Ogden did not note "tribal" boundaries. Ogden then would have been among Athapascan-speaking groups: the Upper Umpqua to the north and the Dakubetede of the Applegate Valley to the southwest. Despite the wide linguistic differences between the Takelma and their Athapascan neighbors, Ogden's journal failed to differentiate between the various native groups; they are all simply "Indians."

Aside from the topic of aboriginal boundaries, Ogden's journal gives additional firsthand information that could be helpful to archaeologists and others. For instance, by Ogden's account, Euro-American (probably Hudson's Bay Company) trade goods had arrived at least as far south and inland as the upper Rogue River drainage by no later than the mid-1820s. His journal documents that Takelma lodges (whatever their actual dimensions may have been) were indeed rectangular, plank structures at the time of Euro-American contact, a question about which there has been some archaeological speculation. The journal's other ethnographic descriptions, although brief, may aid in interpreting the lifeways of the local Indians. Ogden's comments on the "starving" state of many of the Indians, for example, might stimulate archaeological inquiry into the broad question of contact period demographics and the carrying-capacity of local food resources. Additionally, his mention of the many "new Graves" in the Rogue-Umpqua drainages (March 28) may provide a clue to the speed at which Old World diseases had spread from the lower Columbia or coast to other regions.

Geographic Names: The Confusing Case of "Shasta"

PETER OGDEN was not one to go through the countryside bestowing names on every river and peak in sight. Quite the reverse was true; the chief trader generally saved such honors only for the most notable landmarks (for example, the "Clammitte River"), and even then he left a number of major natural features unnamed, and others he failed to mention at all. This was especially true during Ogden's 1826–27 expedition, making it doubly ironic that two of the crucial geographic place-names he *did* give have been misidentified for so long. The river that Ogden named "Sastise" (or "Sasty") was neither the Little Applegate, the Applegate, nor (as one early commentator claimed) the Pit River.[72] Nor was it the northward-draining tributary of the Klamath that presently bears the name Shasta River. Ogden's "Sastise River" was the Rogue River of today, named by him on February 14, the day the brigade first reached its banks. By the same token, Ogden's "Mount Sastise" (misspelled "Sistise" in the surviving copy of his journal) was not the same mountain that has been called "Mount Shasta" for the past century-and-a-half. As discussed in the previous commentary (December "26" and February "15"), Ogden gave this name to the Cascade Range's next large peak to the north, the extinct volcano that has been known to local residents variously as "Mount Clear View," "Snowy Butte," "Mount Pitt," and—as it is now officially named— "Mount McLoughlin."[73] Ethnologist C. Hart Merriam discussed the original place-name history in a 1926 article.[74] Merriam somehow was able to interpret correctly some of Ogden's route, using only the ambiguous 1910 "Laut-Elliott" version of the journal. He briefly traced the ensuing map-making errors, the transposition of the names of Mount Shasta and Pit Mountain ("Mt. Pitt") from their original namesakes, and concluded:

> It is one of the tragedies of geographic nomenclature that [the name "Shasta"], by reason of a break in the continuity of local knowledge of the region, [has] been transferred to features remote from those upon which [it was] originally bestowed. Still, it is something to be thankful for—from the standpoint of anthropology—that both the great mountain and the river to which the name was transferred are still within or bordering on the territory of the Shaste [Shasta] tribe.[75]

This southwesterly view from the left bank of the
Williamson River shows Upper Klamath Lake and snow-
capped Mt. McLoughlin (Abbot's "Mt. Pitt" and Odgen's
"Mt. Sistise"["Sastise"]). Abbot, who travelled in the reverse direction of Ogden's trek, had the advantage of clear
August weather. When Ogden passed along this same spot
nearly thirty years before, it was during a mid-December
storm; the mountain evidently was not visible to him on
this day. (Plate IV, "Mount Pitt, Klamath River and
upper Klamath Lake from Camp 30," in Lt. Henry L. Abbot's report on the 1855 railroad survey, Oregon Historical
Society collections, neg. no. 74163)

When, why and by whom was Ogden's "Mount Sastise" name of 1827
transferred to the California peak? Alexander Roderick McLeod, who
travelled through the same area two years later, most likely was the cul-
prit. In his report to Chief Factor John McLoughlin regarding the route of
the 1829 expedition to the Sacramento Valley, McLeod mentioned that

his party resumed travel on November 29 and "ascertained the track to the base of Chaste Mount."[76] By McLeod's own account, the 1829 brigade was definitely within the upper Pit River drainage during the last week of November. Consequently, his "Chaste Mount" must have referred to the nearby Mount Shasta of today. The cause for McLeod's apparent confusion over the location of Ogden's peak is especially puzzling, considering that his guide was none other than Thomas McKay, the "clerk" who had assisted Ogden on the 1826–27 hunt. Perhaps the original "Mount Sastise" was obscured by clouds when McLeod passed southwards through the Rogue River Valley in early 1829, and McKay failed to notify him of its

---

Portion of Capt. Hood's 1838 map (based directly on J. Arrowsmith's 1834 map), "containing the latest information" provided by the Hudson's Bay Company. Note that the "Shasty R." (the Rogue, Ogden's "Sastise") is mapped as a tributary of the "Clamet," and "M. Shasty" (located just west of "Clamet L.") is today's Mt. McLoughlin. The fold-mark that runs north-south bisects the unnamed peak south of the "Clamet"; this is today's Mt. Shasta. To make matters more complicated, the map's "M. McLoughlin" is one of peaks now known as the Three Sisters! (From Carl Wheat's *Mapping the Transmississippi West*, 1958)

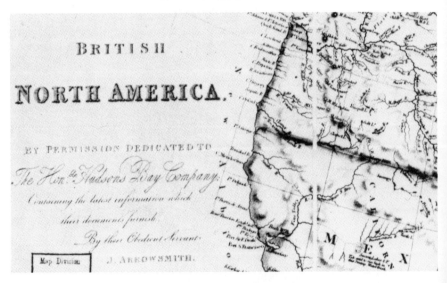

actual location. Whatever the reasons, it is certain that the eventual place-name of Mount Shasta was misapplied quite early in the exploration of the region. Nevertheless, the present Mount Shasta has been "Mount Shasta" for over 150 years—and "Mount Shasta" it no doubt shall remain.[77]

The "Arrowsmith Map" and Early Pacific Northwest Cartography

THE HISTORY of Pacific Northwest geographic names is linked closely to that of the area's early cartography. The steady spread of named places across the map of the region resulted from the explorations of Lewis and Clark, David Thompson, Peter Ogden and others. Ogden's extensive travels south of the Columbia River drainage during the late 1820s provided mapmakers with the first documented accounts of that locality's geography. London cartographer John Arrowsmith relied heavily on Ogden's written testimony (which probably included accompanying sketch maps) in preparing his influential 1834 "Map of the British North America."[78] Arrowsmith's map showed "Mt. Sasty" located well north of the 42nd Parallel (the later Oregon-California boundary) and close to the northwest shore of "Clamet Lake" (Upper Klamath Lake); this would be the approximate location of present Mt. McLoughlin. Arrowsmith also joined the "Clamet" (Klamath) and the "Sasty" (Rogue) Rivers a short distance before they reached the Pacific, and he showed a large (but *unnamed*) peak south of the Klamath River, at the location of today's Mount Shasta. It is obvious that Arrowsmith utilized Ogden's 1826–27 journal (complete with its erroneous references to conjoined drainage systems) for the basic geography of southwestern Oregon-northern California.

Captain Washington Hood based his 1838 map of the region largely on the Arrowsmith version. It retained the imaginary confluence of the Klamath and Rogue Rivers, and it kept the name "Mt. Shasty" at the location of present Mt. McLoughlin. However, Hood added the name "Pit Mountain" to Arrowsmith's unnamed peak (obviously because of its location near the Pit River), today's Mt. Shasta.[79] By the early 1840s, mapmakers had transposed the name Shasta ("Mt. Shaste" on the Wilkes Expedition map) to its present location, but not until several years later did they correctly show the Klamath and Rogue as entirely separate streams.

Due to Arrowsmith's perceived cartographic mistake in combining the Klamath-Rogue drainages, his geographic knowledge of the region has been described as "confused." He also has been criticized for mis-mapping the location of Mount Shasta.[80] True, the rivers of the area proved to follow much different courses through the coastal mountains than his 1834 map showed, but Arrowsmith's confusion in this matter was simply a result of Ogden's understandably ambiguous journal entries. As for the question of misplaced mountains, it was the later commentators who were confused. Arrowsmith located his "Mt. Shasty" in the correct spot—at the actual peak Ogden had christened "Sastise." Most historians have failed to realize that the real geographic error probably was made by Alexander McLeod, or some other early visitor, compounded by later cartographers. Arrowsmith's map was an accurate reflection of the data and assumptions that were available to him from Ogden's 1826–27 journal.

Blazing the "California Trail"

FOR MUCH OF THE WAY between the Willamette Valley and central California, Interstate 5, which crosses Siskiyou Summit just south of Ashland, closely parallels the original Hudson's Bay Company trail of the 1830s. The "HBC Trail" or "California Trail" evolved into the major north-south travel route between the Oregon settlements and the Sacramento Valley, serving in turn everyone from the trappers, government explorers, settlers, gold seekers, and railroad builders of the nineteenth century to the tourists and truckers of the late twentieth.

Today, Siskiyou Summit still remains the most "challenging" mountain pass along the West Coast's entire north-south travel route between British Columbia and Mexico. Nevertheless, it provides the most direct link between the densely settled sections of California and the Pacific Northwest. And, in its own way, Siskiyou Summit proved to be just as geographically significant for the historical development of these two areas as the more famous South Pass, over the Continental Divide, proved to be for the *original* Euro-American migration to these same places. The honor of "first over the Siskiyou Summit" usually has gone, by default, to Alexander McLeod. Because of the subsequent cloud of confusion over the 1826–27 brigade's route, Ogden's claim to this distinction has been almost forgotten. It is now apparent that McLeod's 1829–30 expedition merely retraced Ogden's path south through the Rogue River drainage and over the mountains to the Klamath River.

McLeod's report on his 1829–30 hunt was written at Fort Vancouver, largely in an attempt to justify his poor performance to his superiors.[81] Although this after-the-fact narrative leaves much to be desired in the way of geographic description, McLeod included just enough information for us to follow his route in a general way.

Guided by Thomas McKay from the Umpqua River to the Rogue River,[82] the McLeod brigade proceeded "along said River to a Fork coming from the Southward." Some historians have interpreted this fork as being the Applegate River,[83] but far more likely it was Bear Creek, which

McLeod ascended and then passed "over a height of land to the Clametti River which [he] followed." This places McLeod directly on Ogden's earlier trail.

McLeod ascended the "Clametti," still on Ogden's path, "to the lake." Although this was probably a reference to Upper Klamath Lake, the expedition also must have passed along or near Tule Lake because by late March McLeod had reached the upper Pit River. From this point, McLeod finally diverged from Ogden's 1826–27 track, descending the Pit River into the Sacramento Valley to trap during the spring, summer and fall of 1829. McLeod returned via this same general route to the Rogue River. The resulting large eastward "kink" in the HBC's California Trail (i.e, the detour along the upper Klamath and Pit Rivers) evidently was eliminated by the Laframboise and Work expeditions of 1832–33; after that time, most north-south travellers used the much shorter route that passed west of Mount Shasta.

≶   ≶   ≶

THE CRUCIAL LINK in the California Trail was the section over the Rogue-Klamath divide, the barrier of the Siskiyous. The credit for blazing this portion of the route actually belongs to Peter Skene Ogden. Ogden's stock among Pacific Northwest historians has remained high, and his reputation certainly has not suffered because of this relatively minor oversight.[84]

Master explorer, leader of the wide-ranging "Snake Country Brigades," successor to Dr. John McLouglin as chief factor at Fort Vancouver, rescuer of the Whitman Massacre captives—Peter Skene Ogden played a major role in the drama of the Old Oregon Country. Still, if simple accuracy is one of the primary goals of the historian's craft, the record should reflect Ogden's full contribution to the exploration of southwestern Oregon and northern California. We might do well to remember the begrudgingly favorable comments about Peter Ogden penned by George Simpson in 1832. The acerbic HBC governor, in what was a far from totally flattering assessment, concluded that Ogden's "Services have been so conspicuous . . . that I think he has strong claims to advancement."[85]

NOTES

1. Very probably, at least a few children accompanied their parents. Ogden's Nez Perce wife, Julia, may have been among the women; she is thought to have been with Ogden on some of his other Snake Country journeys, although his journals contain little or no mention of her presence.

On the subject of the chief trader's massive physique, there is little doubt that Peter Ogden's size helped him to impress his will on trapper and native alike. Although in later years he "went to flesh" (the Indians are said to have come to Fort Vancouver especially to view with awe his corpulent physique), Ogden's physical strength was legend. Still, "M'sieu Pete" (as he was dubbed by the French-Canadian trappers) was equally renowned for his intelligence, tact, and sense of humor.

2. T. C. Elliott, ed., "Peter Skene Ogden's Journals: The Journal of Peter Skene Ogden's Snake Expedition, 1826–7," *Oregon Historical Quarterly*, Vol. 11 (1910) 202–29. Laut authored *Conquest of the Great North West* (London 1905), based in part on her research in the HBC's Beaver House archives. The "Laut-Elliott" version of Ogden's journal was used by researchers who realized its severe limitations. Anna Lee Guest ("The Historical Development of Southern Oregon, 1825–1852," M.S. Thesis, Dept. of History, University of California, Berkeley, 1929, p.5) had the following comments:

> from [Ogden's] journal of 1826–27 it is believed that he entered the [Rogue River] territory in February or March 1827. From December 12, 1826 to the fifteenth of May, 1827 his journal is very difficult to follow and the names that he gave to the geographical features are quite confusing. There has been some controversy as to his itinerary, but for his connections with the Rogue River valley, it suffices to say that the authorities agree that he trapped in this region for a short time in the spring of 1827.

3. K. G. Davies, ed., *Peter Skene Ogden's Snake Country Journal, 1826–1827*, intro. by Dorothy O. Johansen (London: Hudson's Bay Record Society, 1961). Excerpts from this volume are reprinted with the permission of the Hudson's Bay Record Society.

4. Richard Dillon, *Siskiyou Trail: The Hudson's Bay Company Route to California* (New York: McGraw-Hill Book Company, 1975). Dillon's book, aimed at a general audience, faithfully follows the 1961 version's route for Ogden, embellishing it with well-written prose that describes the countryside. *See also:* Doyce B. Nunis, Jr., ed., *The Hudson's Bay Company's First Fur Brigade to the Sacramento Valley: Alexander McLeod's 1829 Hunt* (Fair Oaks, California: Sacramento Book Collector's Club, 1968). A second popular work that seems to have incorporated the 1961 route is: Archie Binns, *Peter Skene Ogden: Fur Trader* (Portland: Bindfords and Mort, 1967) 199. *See also:* Samuel N. Dicken and Emily F. Dicken, *The Making Of Oregon: A Study in Historical Geography* (Portland: Western Imprints, 1979) 56–57. Recent works in local history that have uncritically utilized the 1961 route include the "cultural resource overviews" published by federal agencies such as the Bureau of Land Management and the USDA-Forest Service. For example, *see:* Jeffrey M. LaLande, *Prehistory and History of the Rogue River National Forest: A Cultural Resource Overview* (Medford: Rogue River National Forest, 1980) 65–66.

5. It is not felt that these are erroneous interpretations, but the reader should refer to the 1961 edition for its faithful transcription of the original journal's full text.

6. In his preface to the 1961 edition, K.G. Davies documents the fact that the single known surviving copy of the 1826–27 journal actually was the product of someone other than Ogden himself, probably a clerk at Fort Vancouver whose duties included copying field journals for shipment back to Company headquarters in London. *See:* Davies, ed., *Snake Country Journal, 1826–27*, p.x. In their introduction to Ogden's 1827–28 and 1828–29 Journals, Messrs. Miller and Miller also point out that:

> the available journals were not written in Ogden's hand, but were copied by an unidentified Company clerk. This may account for some of the discrepancies in direction and distance—especially direction. Often the direction of travel given in a journal entry does not correspond with that of the preceding or following day's given direction, and does not match the terrain covered. Many of these listings are simply impossible.

See: Glyndwr Williams, ed., *Peter Skene Ogden's Snake Country Journals, 1827–1828 and 1828–1829*, intro. by David E. Miller and David H. Miller (London: Hudson's Bay Record Society, 1971) xxxvii. The same comments would apply to the 1826–27 Journal as well.

Directional errors seem to be common in other early trappers' journals as well. The editor of Jedediah Smith's 1826–27 journal comments on similar discrepancies in the sole surviving copy, a transcription prepared by Smith's St. Louis employee Samuel Parkman; *See:* George R. Brooks, ed., *The Southwest Expedition of Jedediah S. Smith: His Personal Account of the Journey to California, 1826–1827* (Glendale, California: The Arthur S. Clark Company, 1977), 49, n.36.

7. The Williamson River is identified incorrectly as the Sprague River in the 1961 edition.

8. Ethnographer Leslie Spier records the "Barclay Spring" village as being called "di'tk!aks." *See* Leslie Spier, "Klamath Ethnography," *University of California Publications in American Archaelogy and Ethnology #10* (Berkeley: University of California, 1930), 19.

9. Professor Johansen's comment that the "Box wood"-like plant was mountain mahogany is probably a correct identification. (*See:* Davies, ed., *Peter Skene Ogden's Snake Country Journal, 1826–1827*, lxxi.) Curlleaf mountain mahogany (*Cercocarpus ledifolius*) is common on the higher ridges of south-central Oregon. Ogden would have seen this plant during the earlier part of his trek. I do not know of any curlleaf mountain mahogany presently growing along the east edge of Upper Klamath Lake, but the much higher elevation summit

of nearby Naylox Mountain would provide typical habitat. Ogden's comment on the vegetation this day further reinforces the likelihood that the brigade travelled south*east*, over the crest of the steep-faced fault block.

10. The 1961 edition suggests that Ogden was describing the Link River, within the city limits of Klamath Falls, but this would be incompatible with Ogden's course directions, distances, and descriptions since leaving Upper Klamath Lake. This error compounds the geographical confusion over this section of Ogden's route.

11. The large number of Indians whom Ogden mentions for this area, as well as the presence of the fish weir, indicates that the brigade was in the vicinity of the Modoc fishing village of "Tsotso'ksi." *See* Verne F. Ray, *Primitive Pragmatists: The Modoc Indians of Northern California* (Seattle: University of Washington Press, 1963), 211.

12. Carroll Howe, Klamath County resident, Indian relic collector and author; personal communication.

13. In her introduction to the 1961 edition, Professor Johansen states that between December 23 and New Year's Eve, Ogden "literally wandered through the flats of Alturas County [Modoc County, California] between swamp lands and the formidable barrier of the lava country in present Lava Beds National Monument"(xlix). Ogden's journey through this portion of Modoc County was actually a fairly straight march south to Tule Lake and a short distance beyond it to the southwest. Although he would have seen the Medicine Lake Highlands (and Thomas McKay may well have ascended Mount Dome), Ogden probably did not travel that far south.

14. Ray, *Primitive Pragmatists*, 209.

15. Ray, *Primitive Pragmatists*, 169.

16. Ray, *Primitive Pragmatists*, 208. It is important to note that some of Ogden's December 1826 comments on the absence of trees in the Tule Lake area (and later during his May 1827 trek south from Tule Lake to the Pit River), while valid during his visit, are no longer true. Due to fire suppression efforts beginning in the early twentieth century, much of the original bunchgrass-sagebrush community in this region was invaded by the present stands of juniper trees (Frederick C. Hall, Regional Ecologist, USDA-Forest Service, Portland; personal communication).

17. Ray, *Primitive Pragmatists*, 208.

18. The "Devil's Homestead" section of the Lava Beds is a frothy "aa" lava flow. Ogden's route would have been between the Devil's Homestead on the west and Black Crater on the east, the same general path later taken by the U.S. Army's ill-fated Thomas-Wright patrol during the Modoc War in 1873. Although slow-going, this route is traversable by horses.

19. It is possible, therefore, that the term "New Year's Lake" was applied originally to Bonita Lake, since that was where the main party actually spent that date; however, based on one possible interpretation of Ogden's January "3" entry, the party actually may have returned to Tule Lake by January "2" (the actual New Year's Day), 1827.

20. Devere Helfrich, "Peter Skene Ogden's Route Through Klamath County Traced," *Herald and News* (Klamath Falls, February 27, 1970), D-14.

21. Lower Klamath Lake is now largely drained and converted into farmland.

22. Helfrich, "Peter Skene Ogden's Route," D-14.

23. This was probably the village of "iwau'wone," on the Link River in present Klamath Falls. See: Spier, *Klamath Ethnography*, 19.

24. This Beaver Creek is not to be confused with the Beaver Creek which flows into Copco Lake reservoir, much farther upstream.

25. Helfrich, "Peter Skene Ogden's Route," D-14, traces a very similar route for Ogden from the Klamath River crossing west to the Copco Lake area. But from that point (which is beyond his Klamath County area of personal interest) Helfrich defers to the 1961 version of Ogden's trail.

26. The 1961 version would place this point at about Iron Gate Reservoir, much too far downstream.

27. According to Oregon State Department of Fish and Wildlife records, before Copco Dam was built in the early twentieth century a hardy few chinook salmon commonly would ascend beyond the Big Bend Canyon each year—some of them reaching Upper Klamath Lake and the Williamson River. However, the major portion of the annual spawning runs did not pass above the canyon; during some years channel conditions evidently blocked all of the fish from upstream passage.

28. No native sycamores ("Wild Plane Trees") grow in this region, and it is unclear what tree Ogden was referring to here. He could have meant the black hawthorn (*Crataegus douglasii*), which grows in the open areas of the southern Cascades, or bigleaf maple (*Acer macrophyllum*), the leaves of which are similar to sycamore and would have been first encountered by Ogden in this vicinity. Perhaps "Wild Plane Trees" was actually a mis-copy for wild *plum* trees; the Klamath plum (*Prunus subcordata*) does grow in the general vicinity. It is evident, however, that the "stones" Ogden mentioned in this entry referred to the local soil, not to the fruit of these trees. Had it not been winter he might have been moved to comment on the locale's abundant poison oak (*Rhus diversiloba*), the first occasion he would have encountered the plant on the 1826–27 journey.

29. This frustrating tendency of the southern Cascades' "montmorillonite" soils to impede wet-weather travel would plague Ogden and his trappers until after they had crossed the Siskiyou Summit.

30. If, instead of turning south, back towards the river, Ogden had continued westward across the plateau for several more leagues, his scouts might well have discovered the upper Bear Creek Valley by paralleling the later route of the Applegate Trail and present Highway 66.

31. At this hut they met three Shasta women, who were understandably fearful of Ogden's companions; his Klamath guide had killed their husbands during a raid the previous summer.

32. Ogden's "large Fork" is Lost River, which Ogden mistakenly still believed drained into the Klamath.

33. These would have been the villages of "Okwayis" and "Ko-ha'-pi-rah" respectively. See Robert F. Heizer and Thomas R. Hester, "Shasta Villages and Territory" *Contributions of the University of California Archaeological Research Facility* No. 9 (Berkeley: University of California, 1970), 119.

34. The Beaver Creek drainage, in contrast, is covered by a dense forest of Douglas-fir and other conifers; its thin soils are derived from various metamorphic rock types and are not particularly "muddy," at least not in comparison to the volcanic clays of the east half of the Cottonwood Valley.

35. Payette's possible intended crossing point was well to the west, over the high crest of the Siskiyous west of Mt. Ashland.

36. It served as the path for later Hudson's Bay Company trapping brigades; by the 1850s it had evolved into the route of the major wagon road between Oregon and California.

37. Bear Creek Valley forms one major arm of the Rogue River Valley. Other sections include the Agate Desert-Little Butte Creek Valley area, Sams Valley, and—depending on how inclusive one chooses to be—the valley that contains the city of Grants Pass. Together, these make up the Rogue River Valley or "Rogue Valley."

The term "Siskiyou Mountains" once was applied to the entire chain of rugged country between the Klamath River and upper Bear Creek. This included the volcanic mountains of the Pilot Rock-Soda Mountain area that, geologically, are properly included as part of the Cascade Range. Geologists prefer to limit the term "Siskiyous" to the section of the far older Klamath Mountain Province located west of Bear Creek, south of the Rogue River and north of the Klamath River. Ogden's crossing point at "Siskiyou Summit," then, would actually be at the geological contact between the Jurassic Age granitic rocks of the Siskiyou Mountains and the much younger volcanic deposits of the western Cascades.

38. Ogden's reference to "our party of last year," may be to Finan McDonald's trapping expedition into the Klamath Basin.

39. Although his journal does not note the fact (his Shasta guide may have neglected to mention it), Ogden's February "10" bivouac was someplace close to (but probably across Bear Creek from) a geothermal spring known today as Jackson Hot Springs.

40. Although now wooded largely with oak, the lower slopes of the Bear Creek Valley once had many open groves of mature ponderosa pine; most of these were cut down soon after the arrival of American settlers in the 1850s.

41. Although there has been controversy about the location of their northern territorial limits, there was definitely a "Bear Creek Valley band" (the "Ikiruksu") of Shasta. Their lands would have included the southern part of the valley (Neil Creek and Emigrant Creek drainages) and may have extended north at least to Ashland; according to some informants, it even included the Jacksonville area as well. However, Upland Takelma informants disputed this claim and were emphatic that Takelma territory went as far south as Ashland. For more on these questions see: Joel V. Berreman, "Tribal Distribution in Oregon," Memoir No.47 (Menasha: American Anthropological Association, 1937); Roland B. Dixon, "The Shasta," Bulletin No.17 (New York: American Museum of Natural History, 1907); John P. Harrington, The Papers of John Peabody Harrington in the National Anthropological Archives of the Smithsonian Institution, 1907–1957 (Millwood: Krause International Publications, 1981); Robert F. Heizer, Languages, Territories and Names of California Indian Tribes (Berkeley: University of California Press, 1966); Catherine Holt, "Shasta Ethnography," Anthropological Records, Vol. 3:4 (Berkeley: University of California, 1946); Edward Sapir, "Notes on the Takelma Indians of Southwestern Oregon," American Anthropologist, Vol. 9:2 (Menasha: American Anthropological Association, 1907).

42. There is a very slight possibility that the "domesticated Cat" the trapper reported was actually a ring-tail cat (Bassariscus astutus), a relative of the racoon, here found on the northern fringe of its natural range. Ring-tails are easily tamed creatures, and they were popular pets with the early gold miners; perhaps some of the local Indians kept them as well.

43. Quaking aspen (Populus tremuloides) does not now occur along this stretch of the Rogue River; it does grow along the uppermost reaches of the river, above the Union Creek area.

Ogden saw the tree-lined banks of the Rogue in mid-February, well before the leaves had begun to grow. His "Aspines" were probably the locally common red alder (*Alnus rubra*).

44. As Professor Johansen points out in her introduction, Ogden's reference to the mountain's "bearings by our Compass" is puzzling, since by the chief trader's own account, on November "14" Thomas McKay had "lost the onely compass we had" while scouting the sagebrush desert of central Oregon. Ogden made no later mention of the instrument having been found. Perhaps another member of the brigade had included a compass among his personal belongings, and this was then used by Ogden during the trip. Still, February "15" is the single entry subsequent to mid-November that Ogden mentions using a compass.

45. The question of the naming of "Mt. Sastise" (Mt. McLoughlin vs. Mt. Shasta) is discussed in notes 73 and 74, following. However, it is important to note here that I am not the only person to believe that Ogden was referring to present Mt. McLoughlin (which, to confuse matters even more, formerly was known for many years to southwest Oregon residents as "Mt. Pitt"; and the various "folklore" explanations for the origin of that particular name are numerous indeed). C. Hart Merriam came to this same conclusion over half a century ago, in "Source of the Name Shasta," (*Journal of the Washington Academy of Sciences*, 16 (Washington, D.C., 1926) 522–25). *See also* note 74, following.

46. If Ogden's journal *had* mentioned the Table Rocks, the 1961 edition probably would have traced a much more realistic travel route; Ogden's characteristically taciturn writing, in this specific instance at least, definitely contributed to the eventual historiographical mistakes.

47. These were probably Upland Takelma ("Latgawa") from the vicinity of the Table Rocks or Little Butte Creek. Ogden's horrified account of the Indians "like a pack of Wolves . . . devouring the entrils as they were taken out of the Animals Body" is substantiated by Edward Sapir's ethnography (*Notes on the Takelma Indians*, 1907, p.260). Sapir recounts that raw deer fat ("yamx") was considered a "choice part" of Takelma cuisine.

48. Ogden's comment on the large size of Takelma lodges would seem to be at variance with the apparently smaller houses described by Sapir (*Notes on the Takelma Indians*, 1907, p.255). However, there can be little doubt that Ogden was describing rectangular, plank-sided structures generally similar to those documented by Sapir, and not the relatively small, circular pit-houses so far revealed by archaeological excavations in the Rogue River drainage.

49. This environmental contrast still remains very apparent along the Rogue River between Gold Hill and Grants Pass.

50. Artifacts of Chinese manufacture, largely coins and ceramics, have been archaeologically documented for several Oregon aboriginal villages and burial sites. Many of these items undoubtedly arrived among the Indians via European and American trading ships of the late eighteenth and early nineteenth centuries, although some items may have resulted from the shipwreck of an earlier Spanish galleon.

51. *See* Professor Johansen's editorial comments in "Journal of a Hunting Expedition to the Southward of the Umpqua under the command of A.R. McLeod C.T. September 1826," (Appendix C in: Davies, ed., *Peter Skene Ogden's Snake Country Journal, 1826–27* 1961), 175–219. Regarding the identity of Ogden's "Umpqua Chief," Johansen believes this was one of the two Umpqua Indian headmen who accompanied part of McLeod's 1826–27 expedition, and not McLeod himself. Although Ogden did not refer to McLeod by name in these entries, his term "Umpqua Chief" more likely referred to the *Chief* Trader of the HBC's Umpqua Brigade.

52. By now the brigade had taken a little over a thousand pelts, still well under the fifteen-hundred minumum needed for the expedition to be considered a successful one.

53. If, as seems quite likely, Ogden crossed the Rogue near the center of Grants Pass, this would account for his succeeding course directions of west-northwest and northwest.

54. Unless Ogden was taking compass readings from magnetic north without compensating for the local 20° east-of-true-north declination; however, for most other sections his directions seem more accurate.

55. According to some local "old timers," many of the area's Indian trails characteristically followed the crest of ridges, no matter how precipitous the grade might be, and these routes often involved numerous sections of very steep travel. For example, *see* Smith C. Bartrum, "History of Early Forest Work," (Roseburg: personal memoir, n.d.; copy held in Rogue River National Forest historical records collection, item L–18).

56. *See* note 44, above. McLeod's travels certainly included much of the Coquille drainage, as well as that of the Umpqua, near present Roseburg. The Depaty-Laframboise sub-party completed its southward trek before Chief Trader McLeod had made his appearance at the Lookingglass Valley rendezvous camp in February 1827.

57. Jean Baptiste Gervais first arrived in the HBC's Columbia Department in 1823. He was one of the deserters from Ogden's 1825 brigade, but he returned to the fold a short time later. Although his arrival at Fort Vancouver in 1827 is mentioned in McLoughlin's correspondence, no trace of the "letter" Ogden entrusted to Gervais has been found (p.100, n.1 in: Davies, ed., *Peter Skene Ogden's Snake Country Journal, 1826–27*, 1961). *See also*: E. E. Rich, ed., *The Letters of John McLoughlin from Fort Vancouver to the Governor and Committee, First Series 1825–1838*, (London: The Champlain Society for the Hudson's Bay Record Society, 1941), 44–45.

58. The somewhat puzzling description, "cross'd over a point of land," must refer to the Coquille-Cow Creek divide, much more easily ascended from the west than the east. The "River we camped on" probably refers to Cow Creek.

59. The only way to account for Ogden's idea of crossing the Cascade Range via the upper South Umpqua would be that he intended to reach Upper Klamath Lake or Klamath Marsh and there rendezvous with McKay.

60. As pointed out in the "Conclusions" section of this book, the 1834 Arrowsmith Map (and the later maps based on it) clearly reflects Ogden's influence in its joining of the area's various river systems into one larger watershed.

61. In his haste during the southward march over the Siskiyous, Ogden again failed to mention the presence of any large mountain (present Mt. Shasta) visible in the distance.

62. Ray, *Primitive Pragmatists*, 211.

63. Much of the day's journey would have very closely paralleled present California Highway 139.

64. The 1838 map of Capt. Washington Hood, USA (which was based largely on the Arrowsmith Map) shows a large mountain near the headwaters of the Pit River as "Pit Mountain." This was the Mt. Shasta of today. *See* Carl I. Wheat, *Mapping the Transmississippi West*, Vol.2 (San Francisco: The Institute of Historical Cartography, 1958), 146–48, 160–62. The 1961 edition of Ogden's journal interprets his reference to the "*fine* looking River" as meaning Turner Creek, but I do not think this is correct; the brigade easily would have made the right bank of Pit River by midday from their previous encampment.

65. *See* sources listed in note 42, above.

66. For a brief discussion of this question, *See:* Joanne Marylynne Mack, "Archaeological Investigations of the Salt Caves Locality: Subsistence Variability and Cultural Diversity Along the Klamath River, Oregon," (Eugene: Ph.D. dissertation, Department of Anthropology, University of Oregon, 1979).

67. Based on her interpretation of archaeological evidence, Joanne Mack ("Archaeological Investigations of the Salt Caves Locality," 1979, 3) states that the Big Bend Canyon-Salt Caves area likely would have been *Takelma* territory, but I believe this hypothesis conflicts both with most of the ethnographies *and* with Ogden's account (that the area would have been the upstream limit of Shasta territory).

68. *See* Ogden's journal entries for December "26," January "24" and February "1."

69. *See* especially Ogden's journal entries for February "10" and "15."

70. *See* Ogden's journal entry for February "13."

71. However, both the Upland Takelma and the Shasta may well have used the land between these two places on an intermittent or shared basis (possibly for visits to the geothermal springs at Jackson Hot Springs?). Molly Orton (a.k.a. Orcutt), John Harrington's Upland Takelma informant, mentioned her people's use of Jackson Hot Springs. *See* Harrington, *The Papers of John Peabody Harrington*, 1981.

72. Elliott, ed., "The Journal of Peter Skene Ogden: Snake Expedition, 1826–7," 1910, 213, n.3.

73. The first known use of the name "Pit Mountain," was on Hood's 1838 map of the Pacific Northwest. The location was virtually the same as that of *today's* Mount Shasta, obviously due to this peak's proximity to the Pit River. Some years later, because of the earlier misappropriation of the name "Mount Shasta" for the California mountain, the name "Pit Mountain" (although it was given added "dignity" with an extra "t" and transposition of the words into "Mount Pitt") was applied to the Oregon peak (present Mount McLoughlin), far from the sources of the Pit River! *See:* Carl I. Wheat, *Mapping the Transmississippi West*, Vol. 2, (1958), 160–62.

74. Merriam, "Source of the Name Shasta," 1926, 522–25. When Merriam wrote this paper, Mt. McLoughlin was still commonly referred to as "Mount Pitt," hence his use of that term (many long-time local residents continue to use that name).

75. Merriam, "Source of the Name Shasta," 525.

76. Nunis, ed., *The Hudson's Bay Company's First Fur Brigade to the Sacramento Valley: Alexander McLeod's 1829 Hunt*, 1968, 39.

77. Even if there had not been a misuse of the name "Shasta" for another peak, Mount McLoughlin is certainly no candidate for yet *another* name. Considering the succession of subsequent names bestowed on this particular mountain (Mt. Clear View, Snowy Butte, Mt. John Quincy Adams, Mt. Pitt, Mt. McLoughlin) it would be absurd to complicate matters by rechristening it with its first historic name. However, it would be appropriate, if and when this "revised Ogden route" becomes generally accepted, to correct history textbooks, point-of-interest roadsigns, historical maps and similar public information. (For example, the bronze plaque fastened to the wall of the Sierra Club's "Horse Camp" Alpine Lodge, elevation 7,800 ft., on Mt. Shasta's south slope credits Ogden with "discovering" that Mt. Shasta on February 14, 1827.)

78. Wheat, *Mapping the Transmississippi West*, Vol. 2 (19580, 146–48. *See also*: Clarence R. Allen, "The Myth of the Multnomah: The History of a Geographical Misconception," *Reed College Bulletin*, Vol. 27:4 (Portland: Reed College, 1949), 91–113.

79. *See* Wheat, *Mapping the Transmississippi West*, Vol. 2 (1958), 160–62 and plate 433.

80. Dillon, *The Siskiyou Trail*, 1975, p.147. Wheat, *Mapping the Transmississippi West*, Vol. 2 (19580, 148.

81. Nunis, *The Hudson's Bay Company's First Fur Brigade to the Sacramento Valley: Alexander McLeod's 1829 Hunt*, 1968.

82. Probably McLeod's "Sarti" (a mis-copy for "Sasti"?). McLeod's report contains a bewildering number of spellings for what may or may not have been separate rivers and valleys (e.g., "Sarti," "Sasti," "Chaste," and even "Nastey"!).

83. Nunis, *The Hudson's Bay Company's First Fur Brigade to the Sacramento Valley: Alexander McLeod's 1828 Hunt*, 1968, 45, n.1–3.

84. In the past, some American historians have shown an unconsciously nationalistic tendency to ignore (or at least to minimize) the scope and importance of geographic exploration undertaken by the Hudson's Bay Company in the Far West. One unusually recent example of this view of regional history is in *An Historical Atlas of Early Oregon*, by Judith A. Farmer and Kenneth L. Holmes (Portland: Historical Cartographic Publications, 1973). In the section dealing with "Early Overland Expeditions of Northwest America," the authors show the travel routes of Americans Jedediah Smith (1827–28) and Ewing Young (1836) through northwest California and southwest Oregon, but they include no reference to the previous HBC explorations in the area. Young (who merely followed the trail blazed by Ogden, McLeod and others) is, in essence, presented as the pioneer of the "California-Oregon Trail" over the Siskiyous. The book, which deals with Pacific Northwest explorations up through the 1840s, also fails to discuss Ogden's expeditions across the sagebrush plains of central Oregon; incredibly, the *Atlas* contains not a single mention of Ogden's name.

85. Glyndwr Williams, ed., "The Character Book of George Simpson, 1832," *Hudson's Bay Miscellany, 1670–1870*, Vol. 30 (Winnipeg: Hudson's Bay Record Society, 1975), 194.

In closing—and as a "final word" on the subject of Peter Ogden's "strong claims to advancement"—it is ironic that southwestern Oregon-northwestern California contains virtually no place-names which commemorate the chief trader and his trek through the region. A trivial matter perhaps, *and* it is true that two short hiking trails along the Army Corps of Engineers' new (1980) Applegate Lake reservoir do recall the memory of Ogden and Payette. But these trails were named in the belief that Ogden had passed near the present reservoir site, that the 1961 route interpretation was correct. A more appropriate monument might simply be to name a portion of Jackson County's Bear Creek Greenway trail, which closely approximates the path of the 1827 brigade, after Ogden; or better yet, the presently unnamed "high hill" just west of Siskiyou Summit (the one Ogden must have climbed to view the Bear Creek Valley) might be christened "Ogden's Hill."

SELECTED BIBLIOGRAPHY

SEVERAL OF THE WORKS listed below are cited in the Notes. The other studies provide valuable background information on the Hudson's Bay Company in the Old Oregon Country.

Davies, K. G., editor. *Peter Skene Ogden's Snake Country Journal, 1826–27,* Introduction by Dorothy O. Johansen (London: Hudson's Bay Record Society, 1961).

Dodds, Gordon B. *The American Northwest: A History of Oregon and Washington* (Arlington Heights, Illinois: Forum Press, 1986).

Elliott, T. C., editor. "Peter Skene Ogden's Journals" The Journal of Peter Skene Ogden's Snake Expedition, 1826–7," *Oregon Historical Quarterly* (1910).

Galbraith, John S., *The Hudson's Bay Company as an Imperial Factor, 1821–1869* (Berkeley: University of California Press, 1957).

Hussey, John A. *The History of Fort Vancouver and Its Physical Structure* ([Tacoma]: Washington State Historical Society, 1957).

Johansen, Dorothy O. and Charles M. Gates. *Empire of the Columbia: A History of the Pacific Northwest* (New York: Harper and Row, 1967).

Lavender, David. "Fort Vancouver and the Pacific Northwest," *Fort Vancouver.* National Parks Handbook 113 (Washington, D.C., National Park Service, n.d.).

MacKay, Douglas. *The Honourable Company: A History of the Hudson's Bay Company* (Toronto: McClelland and Stewart, 1948).

Meinig, D.W. *The Great Columbia Plain: A Historical Geography* (Seattle: University of Washington Press, 1968).

Murray, Keith A. "The Role of the Hudson's Bay Company in Pacific Northwest History." *Experiences in a Promised Land: Essays in Pacific Northwest History.* G. Thomas Edwards and Carlos A. Schwantes, editors (Seattle: University of Washington Press, 1986).

Nunis, Doyce B., Jr., ed. *The Hudson's Bay Company's First Fur Brigade to the Sacramento Valley: Alexander McLeod's 1829 Hunt* (Fair Oaks, California: Sacramento Book Collector's Club, 1968).

Rich, E.E. *The Letters of John McLoughlin from Fort Vancouver to the Governor and Committee, First Series 1825–1838.* (London: Champlain Society for the Hudson's Bay Record Society, 1971).

Wheat, Carl I. *Mapping the Transmississippi West*, 2 (San Francisco: Institute of Historical Cartography, 1958).

Williams, Glyndwr, editor. *Peter Skene Ogden's Snake Country Journals, 1827–1828 and 1828–1829*, Introduction by David E. Miller and David H. Miller (London: Hudson's Bay Record Society, 1971).

INDEX

Abbot, Henry Larcom, 125
Achumawi Indians, 118
Adams Point, 116
Allen Creek, 87, 90, 105
Antelope Creek, 71
Applegate, 106
Applegate Lake, 107
Applegate River, 124, 128; Hudson's Bay
    Record Society edition puts Ogden
    on, 53, 57, 68, 72; Ogden reaches,
    82-84, 86, 95, 97, 104-106; photo,
    105
Applegate Valley, xxxi, 57, 106, 108,
    123; photo, 107
Arrowsmith, John, 105; "Map of British
    North America," 126-27
Ashland, 55, 57, 61, 123, 127; photos,
    59, 60
Ashland Creek, 61

Barkley Spring, 6, 9
Barron, Hugh (house), 55
Beal Mountain, 101
Bear Creek, Jackson Co., 55, 57, 61, 68-
    69, 108, 128; photos, 59, 60, 63
Bear Creek Valley, Jackson Co., xxxi,
    44, 46, 53, 55, 74, 97, 109; described,
    57, 59, 61, 64, 68, 71; Indians, 61,
    62, 64, 68, 122-23; photos, 50, 59,
    65
Beaver Basin, Copco Lake, 41, 43, 44,
    111

Beaver Creek, Siskiyou Co., 31, 49
Beavers: Bear Creek Valley, 61-64;
    Coquille River, 90-92; Cow Creek,
    88, 97, 98, 104; lack of in Klamath
    Falls–Lost River area, 10, 12, 14, 23,
    29; lack of on Klamath River, 43;
    numbers trapped by brigade, 72, 111,
    113; Pit River, 117; Rogue River, 69,
    72, 73, 82, 84-86; Shasta area, 111,
    113, South Umpqua River, 99-100;
    "trap out the streams" policy, xxii,
    xxiv, xxvii
Beswick, Calif., xxviii, 3, 25, 28, 31, 33,
    42, 43, 122
Beswick Hot Springs, Calif., 5, 26-27;
    see also Klamath Hot Springs, Shovel
    Creek Hot Springs
Big Bend Canyon (Klamath River), 33-
    35, 37, 42, 122; photo, 36
Big Dutchman Butte, 90
Big Sugarloaf Peak, 108
Black Mountain, 44
Blackwell Hill, 74, 79
Bloody Point, 15
Board Shanty Creek, 106
Bonita Lake, 19, 21, 133; photo, 21
Brandy Peak, 87
Brush Creek, Siskiyou Co., 44
Buck Butte, Klamath Co., 14
Buck Lake, Klamath Co., 34
Buonaventura River (mythical), xxvii,
    100

146

Butte Valley, 27

California-Oregon Stage Road, 55
Camas Valley, 91-92
Camp Creek, Siskiyou Co., 35, 37
Canby, Calif., 117
Canby Cross, Siskiyou Co., 22, 23
Canyonville, 101
Carberry Creek, 108
Carter Creek, Jackson Co., 55
Cascade Gorge, Jackson Co., 73
Cascade Range, 61, 64, 101
Central Point, 57, 59, 68; photo, 67
Chemult, 29
Chiloquin, 6
Clear Lake, Calif., 13
Clear Lake Reservoir, Calif., 13
Cold Springs, Klamath Co., 9
Copco Lake, 28, 37, 41, 111, 122
Copco Lake Reservoir, 33; photo, 45
Copic Bay, 16, 23, 116; photo, 16
Coquille River, 102, 103, 104; Umpqua
    Brigade on, 82; see also Middle Fork,
    Coquille River
Cottonwood Creek, Calif., xxxi, 33, 35,
    37, 42-44, 49-50, 53, 55, 64, 71, 109;
    photos, 46, 47
Cottonwood Creek Valley, Siskiyou Co.,
    43, 52; photo, 49
Cow Creek, 77, 87-88, 90, 95, 97-98,
    101-104; photo, 89
Crater Lake, Jackson Co., 74
Crescent, 29

Dairy, 11
Dakubetede Indians, 107, 123
Darby Creek, 88, 90, 95, 97
Days Creek, 95, 101
Dead Indian Plateau, 64
Depaty, Jean Baptiste, 82, 99
Dice Creek, 90
Dillon, Richard, xxxi
Dodds Hollow, 116
Dunsmuir, Calif., 113

Elliott, T. C., xxviii, 124
Emigrant Creek, 60, 63, 64, 109
Evans Creek, 80-82, 97, 108

Fish Lake, Jackson Co., 72

Foots Creek, 80
Fort Nez Perce, xxxi, 118
Fort Vancouver, xxi, xxii-xxiv, 29, 91,
    92, 97, 101, 104, 118-19, 128; view,
    xxvii; Warre painting, xxiv
Freemen (independent trappers), xxvii-
    xxviii, 23, 25, 29, 85, 87

Gervais, Jean Baptiste, 91, 92, 97, 103
Gillem Bluff, 18, 19, 23; photos, 17, 18,
    20
Glade Creek, 53, 61
Glendale, 87
Gold Hill, 71, 79, 81
Gold Ray Dam, 68, 74
Goosenest Range, 42
Grants Pass, xxxi, 74, 77, 82, 84-87, 90,
    91, 95, 104; photo, 83
Grave Creek, 86-87, 104
Grayback Mountain, 106, 108; photo, 107
Grizzly Peak, 61

Hackamore, Calif., 116
Happy Camp, Calif., 71
Hayden Mountain Pass, 35
Helfrich, Devere, 25, 29
Hellgate Canyon (Rogue River), 104
Henley, 24, 27, 114
Hill Creek, Jackson Co., 55, 60, 109;
    photos, 50, 55
Hilt, Calif., 52
Hogback Mountain, 11; photo, 8
Hood, Washington, 126, 127
Hopper Hill, 10; photo, 9
Hornbrook, Calif., 35, 50
Horse Mountain, 15
Howards Gulch, 111, 117
Hudson's Bay Company: California trail,
    121-22, 127-28; fur trapping policy in
    Oregon Country, xxii, xxiv, xxvii;
    geographical explorations, 139; trade
    goods, 72, 79-80, 84, 123
Hudson's Bay Record Society, xv, xvii,
    xviii, xxxi
Hungry Hill, 87

Iron Gate Dam, 44
Iron Gate Reservoir, 28, 35, 37

Jackson Hot Springs, 135, 138

Johansen, Dorothy O., xxxi
Jumpoff Joe Creek, 82, 86, 104

Kane Creek, 79
Karok Indians, 71
Keno, 34, 113
Klamath Basin, 101
Klamath-Deschutes divide, 29
Klamath Falls, xxxi, 3, 5, 9, 11, 24-27,
    31, 111, 114, 133; hot springs, 26,
    28-29
Klamath Hot Springs, Calif., 25, 26-27;
    see also Beswick Hot Springs, Shovel
    Creek Hot Springs
Klamath Indians, 6-7, 10, 12, 14, 23,
    28, 29, 33, 34, 37-38, 61, 122
Klamath Marsh, 6, 25, 29
Klamath Mountains, 42, 43
Klamath River, xxix, 11, 13, 24-25, 74,
    109; Arrowsmith map, 127; lower
    river Indians, 71; name, 123-24;
    Ogden crossing site near Klamath
    Falls, xxxi, 3, 5, 28, 29, 31, 33, 111,
    113-14; Ogden description, 28, 34,
    35, 38, 40, 43; Ogden's geographical
    misconception of, 62-63, 68, 77, 82-
    83, 92, 95-96, 104-106, 127; photos,
    26, 27, 46
Klamath River Canyon, 33, 122

Laframboise, Michel, 82, 99, 128
Lake Ewauna, 11, 26, 27
Laut, Agnes C., xxviii, 124
Lava Beds National Monument, 17-19,
    21, 23, 133; photos, 18, 20, 21, 22
Leland, 86
Link River, 11, 25-29, 133
Little Applegate River, xxviii, 31, 53,
    57, 61, 62, 124
Little Butte Creek, 71, 72, 74
Little Shasta River, 113
Long Point, 34
Long Prairie, 37-38, 113; photos, 37,
    115
Long Prairie Creek, 35, 38, 41, 111, 113;
    photo, 39
Lookingglass Valley, 100, 137
Lost River, xxxi, 3, 5, 11-14, 23-24, 34,
    111, 115, 116; Ogden description,
    10, 12; photos, 10, 116

Louse Creek, 86
Lower Klamath Lake, 11, 12, 24-26, 28,
    133; photo, 27
Lower Table Rock, 71; photo, 70

McDonald, Finan, 135
McKay, Thomas, xxvii, 10, 19, 21, 23,
    43, 64, 74, 79, 82, 85, 109, 111, 113,
    116, 124, 128, 133, 136
McKay Flat, Calif., 116, 117
McLeod, Alexander Roderick, 82, 91,
    99, 104, 124, 127, 128, 136-37
McLoughlin, John, xxiv, xxvii, 119,
    124; photo, xxv
Malin, 14, 23; photo, 14
Medford, 57,68
Medicine Lake, 19
Medicine Lake Highlands, 19, 21, 133;
    photos, 17, 117
Meiss Lake, 27
Merlin, 86, 104
Merrill, 116
Merriman, C. Hart, xviii, 124
Middle Fork, Coquille River, xxxi, 77,
    87, 90-92, 95; see also Coquille River
Miners Creek, 108
Missouri Bottom, 98; photo, 99
Modoc Indians, 12-18, 22-23, 114-16,
    122
Modoc Point, 6
Modoc Rim–Naylox Mountain fault
    block, 6, 9; photo, 8
Mount Ashland, 51, 61; photos, 47, 60
Mount Baldy, 61
Mount Dome, 19, 133; photos, 20, 21
Mount McLoughlin, 68, 69; Arrowsmith
    map, 127; Ogden name for, 124;
    photos, 67, 125
Mount Sexton, 86
Mt. Sexton Pass, 86
Mount Shasta, 42-43, 113; Arrowsmith
    map, 127; Hood map, 127; name, 15-
    16, 66-69, 123-25, 127, 128, 136;
    photos, 15, 49
Moyina Hill, 10; photos, 9, 13
Murphy, 106
Murphy Creek, Josephine Co., 106
Myrtle Creek, 95, 99

Naylox Mountain, 133

Neil Creek, 60-61, 63
North Umpqua River, 104; *see also*
South Umpqua River, Umpqua River
North West Company, xxii

Oak Knoll, Calif., 31
Oatman Lake, 34
Ogden, Julia, 131
Ogden, Peter Skene: Arrowsmith use of
maps and journals, 126-27; career,
xxii, 129; geographical sites named
for, 139; portrait, xxix; profile, xxiii;
Snake Country Brigades, xxii, 129;
see also Ogden journal, 1826-27
Ogden journal, 1826-27: confusions in
text, xxviii, 3, 9, 77, 101, 121;
dating, xxxi, xxxvii; Elliott-Laut
1910 version, xxviii, Hudson's Bay
Record Society 1961 publication,
xxviii, xxx, xxxi, xxxvii; "original"
journal, 3; photos, xxxv, xxxvii
Olene, 3
Olene Ford, 12
Olene Gap, 12
Onion Creek, 105

Pacific Ocean: Shasta Indian knowledge
of, 45, 46, 64
Payette, François, xxvii, 18, 24-25, 46,
53, 64, 68, 71, 72, 74, 79
Phoenix, 57, 68
Pilot Rock, Jackson Co., 51; photos, 45,
49
Pine Flat, 10
Pit River, xxxi, 111, 116-17, 124, 127;
name, 118, 128; photo 119
Poe Valley, 14
Pokegama Plateau, 33, 35, 42, 111;
photos, 39, 40
Pollard Station, 87
Preston Peak, Calif., 71
Prospect, xxxi, 57

Raymond Gulch, 41; photo, 40
Red Buttes, Jackson Co., 71
Red Mountain, Jackson Co., 31
Remote, 91
Riddle, 97, 101, 103
Rogue River, xxvii, xxxi, 5, 57, 61, 95,
128; Arrowsmith map, 127;

fluctuations in river level, 71, 79, 80,
108; Ogden description, 65-67, 69,
79, 80, 82, 104, 108; Ogden's
geographical misconception of, 62-
63, 77, 82, 84, 85, 104, 127; Ogden
name for, 66, 124; photos, 66, 73,
81, 83; upper river exploration, 72-74
Rogue River, 81
Rogue River Valley, 44, 45, 59, 124
Ruch, 107

Sacramento River, xxvii, 60, 113, 117
Sacramento Valley, 127-28
Salmon Mountains, 42
Salt Caves, Klamath Co., 34, 122
Sams Creek, 71
Sams Valley, 71
Sand Creek, Josephine Co., 82
Savage Creek, 108
Sawyer, Robert W., xiv
Schroeder Park, Grants Pass, 85
Scotch Creek, Calif., 37
Scott Mountains, 42
Scott River, Calif., 113
Shady Cove, 72
Shasta Indians, 15, 33-35, 40-48 *passim*,
50, 53, 55, 60, 61, 63, 69; knowledge
of Pacific Ocean, 45, 46, 64;
territorial boundaries, 64, 122, 124,
135
Shasta River, 113, 124
Sheep Hill, Douglas Co., 99
Shively Creek, Douglas Co., 103
Shovel Creek Hot Springs, Calif., 25,
27; *see also* Beswick Hot Springs,
Klamath Hot Springs
Simpson, George, xxii, xxiv, 129;
photo, xxvi
Siskiyou Gap, 53; photo, 52
Siskiyou Mountains, xvii, 31, 43, 44, 50-
51, 61, 86, 97, 106, 107, 135;
McLeod crossing, 128; Ogden
crossing, xxi-xxii, xxviii, xxxi, 28,
31, 33, 50-55, 57, 84, 109; Payette
crossing, 135; photos, 47, 48, 59
Siskiyou Peak, 31
Siskiyou Summit, xxxi, 52, 53, 55, 109,
123, 127-29, 135; photos, 48, 51, 62
Snake Country Brigades: purposes, xxii,
xxiv, xxvii

Snake River, xxxi, 118
South Umpqua Falls, 102
South Umpqua River, xxxi, 87, 95, 97-99, 101, 103, 104; photos, 99, 100, 102; see also North Umpqua River, Umpqua River
Spannus Gulch, 41, 42; photo, 40
Spaulding Creek, Jackson Co., 52
Spencer Creek, Klamath Co., 34, 113
Sprague River, 132
Stukel, 24
Stukel Ford, 115, 116; photo, 116
Sugarloaf Mountain, Jackson Co., 87
Swan Lake Valley, 3, 9-11

Table Rocks, 71, 72, 108
Takelma Indians, 79-80, 84-88 passim, 101, 103; territorial boundaries, 122-23, 135; see also Upland Takelma Indians
Talent, 57, 62, 123; photo, 62
Texum, 27
Thompson Creek, 106, 107, 108; photo, 107 .
Tou Velle State Park, 74
Trail Creek, Jackson Co., 57, 72
Tule Lake, Calif., xxxi, 3, 5, 11, 14-18, 22-24, 42, 111, 116, 128, 133
Tule Lake Basin, Calif.: photos, 16, 17, 18, 20
Turner Creek, Calif., 111, 117
Twelvemile Creek, Douglas Co., 90, 91, 97
Two-mile Ridge, 9

Umpqua Brigade, 82, 91, 98-100, 104

Umpqua Indians, 103; see also Upper Umpqua Indians
Umpqua River, 77, 90, 95, 101, 128; see also North Umpqua River, South Umpqua River
Umpqua Valley, 71
Union Creek, Douglas Co., 90
Union Creek, Jackson Co., 73
Upland Takelma Indians, 61, 64-65, 68-72, 123, 136; territorial boundaries, 64; see also Takelma Indians
Upper Klamath Lake, xxii, xxxi, 3, 6, 13, 23-25, 128, 132, 133; photos, 6, 7, 125
Upper Table Rock, 71
Upper Umpqua Indians, 123; see also Umpqua Indians

Wagner Butte, 61, 63; photo, 62
Wagner Creek, 62, 109, 123
Walker Creek, 64
Walker Mountain, 86
Weyerhaeuser mill, Klamath Falls, 26, 28, 29, 33
Whiteline Reservoir, 9
Williams Creek, 106
Williamson River, 6; photo, 5
Willow Creek, Jackson Co., 3, 12, 23-24
Wilson Dam, 114
Wolf Creek, Josephine Co., 87
Women: accompanying fur trapping brigades, xxi, xxviii
Work, John, 128

Yale Creek, 62

COLOPHON

S EVEN DECADES after Frederic W. Goudy designed it, Goudy Old Style remains one of the most popular—and readable—book faces ever produced by an American. The Oregon Historical Society Press has used Goudy Old Style a number of times because of its good design and its legibility, and it is so used in *First Over the Siskiyous* for these same solid reasons. Goudy often stated that he was inspired to this design by letter forms done by Hans Holbein, and the type designer considered the face as one of his most innovative. Goudy Open, used as the display face in this volume—and referred to today as Goudy Handtooled — is another production of the same designer. Goudy felt that he made this face distinct from its historical antecedents (e.g. Bodoni) by "bravely" increasing the weight of the hairlines.

The text of *First Over the Siskiyous* was typeset by the Austin, Texas firm of G&S Typesetters; the index and colophon by Irish Setter and the display by Paul O. Giesey, both Portland firms. Produced in the OHS Press tradition of fine bookmaking, this volume is printed on cream color, wove-finish, seventy-pound Warren Olde Style (a neutral pH paper chosen for its longevity) by the Irwin-Hodson Company, and bound in Holliston Kingston Natural Black Cloth and Papan Maroon Vellum by Lincoln & Allen, again both Portland companies. The endpapers are eighty-pound Oxford Grey Gilbert Oxford Text.

First Over the Siskiyous was edited, designed, and produced by the Oregon Historical Society Press.